STAMP COLLECTORS' HANDBOOK

By FRED REINFELD

Adapted by Burton Hobson

Edited by Robert Obojski

DOUBLEDAY & COMPANY, INC.
GARDEN CITY, NEW YORK

OTHER BOOKS BY FRED REINFELD

CATALOGUE OF THE WORLD'S MOST POPULAR COINS

COIN COLLECTORS' HANDBOOK

Revised Edition
Copyright © 1980, 1976, 1970 by
Sterling Publishing Co., Inc.
Two Park Avenue, New York, N.Y. 10016
A President Coin Publication, published in the United States and Canada by
Doubleday and Company, Garden City, New York
Manufactured in the United States of America
All rights reserved
ISBN 0–385–17077–7
Library of Congress Catalog Card No.: 77-111945

Contents

"Postmasters' Provisionals" were issued in certain cities to facilitate prepayment of postage in the period shortly before regular stamps were introduced in 1847. These envelopes, produced in 1845-46 in various shades of paper for use in Baltimore, were hand-stamped with a 5 (for 5¢) and signed by Baltimore postmaster, James M. Buchanan.

1. A Brief History of the U.S. Postal System

The United States postal system has its roots in the settlement of the Thirteen Colonies. The colonies' growth necessitated a dependable means of communication, and by the end of the 17th century a regular service was established on a monthly basis between New York and Boston on order of the "Master of the Postes" in England. This route, U.S. Highway 1, the oldest and perhaps most famous in the country, is still known by its old name "The Boston Post Road."

In 1683, Governor William Penn of Pennsylvania set up a post office in Philadelphia. Its postmaster had broad powers which permitted him to supply horses for travelers, as well as to send weekly mail between Philadelphia and New Castle, Delaware, on a regular schedule. The schedule of departure was displayed in public places for the information of the population. This was the first time that regular scheduled transportation was used for both travelers and the carrying of mail.

Although William Penn extended the service to other towns, all in Pennsylvania, there was no unified system connecting the colonies from north to south. Early attempts by the Virginia General Assembly to rectify this weakness failed, as the settlements were too scattered.

The early postal routes followed streams or old Indian trails and the riders faced many dangers, not only from Indians, but from settlers for whom the inviolability of the mail had no meaning. Because of the uncertainty of delivery, the custom was to pay on receiving mail, rather than on sending it. This custom lasted well into the 19th century and hampered the efficiency of the postal service, because many abuses resulted, and revenues were always uncertain.

Benjamin Franklin was appointed Postmaster at Philadelphia in 1735. At the same time he was given the task of systematizing the entire Colonial service, and setting up uniform accounting procedures for local postmasters. In 1753, he was appointed Co-Deputy Postmaster General with William Hunter. So thoroughly did they do their job that the postal revenues from the scattered colonies were three times greater than those of Ireland. Although the postal service prospered under him, Benjamin Franklin was dismissed in 1774 because of his sympathy for the American revolutionaries. Without his determined enforcement of the privacy of the mail during the turbulent years preceding the Revolution, the Committees of Correspondence could not have successfully carried out their plans for the meeting in Philadelphia where the Declaration of Independence was ultimately signed.

Before the Revolution, the needs for communication were served by the infrequent post rider carrying letters at a cost of about 75¢ for a single sheet—the equivalent of a days' pay for a farmhand. Now, less than 200 years later, powerful jets carry mail from New York to California in something like five or six hours and the whole United States is served by a Post Office Department with over 500,000 employees, using every means available, from jeep to microwaves, to handle annually what amounts to nearly two-thirds of all the world's mail: over 100 billion pieces of domestic mail of all kinds, and over one billion pieces of international mail.

The United States Post Office Department, which grew so spectacularly over 200 years, became the United States Postal Service, a semi-independent organization, on July 1, 1971. The Postmaster-General is no longer a member of the Cabinet but is appointed by a nine-member Board of Governors which directs the operation.

Even before the Revolution, on July 26, 1775, the Continental Congress passed an act establishing an independent service for the Colonies and appointed Benjamin Franklin Postmaster General with broad powers to organize it. He held the office only 16 months, but the work he did then in reorganizing the service, and the pioneering work he had done in the British Colonial Service, gave him the right to the title of "Father of the United States Postal Service." After the Revolution, the Continental Congress combined its earlier regulations into one law which followed Franklin's suggestion that postal revenues be used for the improvement of the service. Riders were permitted to carry newspapers as mail, and the salaries of postmasters were fixed at not more than one-fifth of their revenues.

6

When the Constitution became the law of the land in 1789, it gave Congress the power to establish post offices and post roads. Congress used this power that year and passed its first postal act, under which President George Washington appointed the first Postmaster General under the Constitution. He took control of a system of about 75 postmasters and 2,000 miles of post roads.

At the start, the Post Office Department was beset with many difficulties. It was not then a separate entity, but was part of the Treasury Department, which at that time was coping with fantastic fiscal difficulties left over from the Revolution. The carrying of the mail was in the hands of contractors and yielded a total annual income of $25,000. To improve service, the Postmaster General had been authorized in 1785 to employ stage coaches, but the condition of the roads was so poor that the coaches made very little difference.

The first Postmaster General appointed by President Washington was Samuel Osgood of Massachusetts, who made a report of what he considered the weaknesses of the system at that time. Alexander Hamilton, Secretary of the Treasury, his superior, passed it on to Congress. Among Osgood's observations were references to the scattered nature of the settlements; the suggestion that the franking privilege (free mail to officials) was excessive; foreign mail was not properly attended to; postage rates were too high in some cases or too low in others; carriers were handling mail privately which should have gone into the regular mail; postmasters did not always consider the public interest before their own. Regarding letters, he estimated that revenues were lost to the post office either because mail was not accepted by the addressee, or the cash-on-delivery fees were pocketed by the carriers.

To remedy these evils, he recommended revision of the rates; strict regulation of postmasters and of riders who were careless about schedules, and who often carried mail and newspapers for private profit; and that postmasters be appointed on the basis of ability. He pointed out that letting contracts for delivery to the lowest bidder resulted in their being given to those least able financially to carry them out.

Osgood also recommended an innovation which was enthusiastically welcomed by postmasters: that there be a charge of from 1¢ to 1½¢ for carrying newspapers, payable in advance, one-half of the receipts to be kept by the postmaster. This was a welcome inducement, as up to then postmasters could keep only one-fifth of the fees collected for letter postage delivered for payment of all expenses. Not only did Osgood's proposal anticipate nationwide prepaid and stamped letter mail by half a century, but the principle of a preferred rate for newspapers has lasted to this day.

Osgood enthusiastically went to work to improve the vital thread of communications by appointing energetic assistants to reform the totally inadequate system in the South and to act as postmasters in the important centers in Philadelphia and New York. So thorough a job was done that by 1795 the number of post offices had increased to 453, the miles of post roads to 13,207, and annual revenue to $160,000.

During the 1790's, postal legislation included a modification of the ancient death penalty for interfering with the mails. Capital punishment, to which there had been no alternative, had rarely been carried out, as juries and judges simply failed to convict a culprit.

Although there was still a need for standards of ethics, and for recognition of the sanctity of the mails, a firm foundation for the extension and development of the postal service had been laid by the end of the 18th century. From that time on, in spite of the poor roads, the service expanded rapidly. In fact, so efficient were the operations during President Jefferson's administration, that he considered using postal profits to reduce the national debt!

During the next decades, the Post Office (which in 1827 became a branch of the government independent of the Treasury) adopted every new means of transportation to speed the carrying of the mail. The use of paddlewheelers, canal boats, and railroads eliminated many of the dangers which had hampered postal operations. A law was passed regulating the method of letting contracts to carriers. This was supposed to reduce the patronage powers of the Postmaster

Robert H. Harris, postmaster at New York City, in July, 1845, was the first to issue adhesive stamps on a regional basis in order to test the practicality of this type of prepaid postage. The New York provisionals (5¢ black with Washington's portrait, as shown) were also used by postmasters at Albany, Boston, Philadelphia, Washington and in several other cities.

This stamp enlarged.

This is a scarce uncut sheet of 12 of the 1846 5¢ black Providence, R.I., Postmaster's Provisional. A similarly-designed 10¢ value was also issued. Since Postmasters' Provisionals were used for only a brief period, they are all quite rare today.

General and to allow for more local autonomy and efficiency. The Postmaster General was authorized to make agreements with foreign countries for the safe, expeditious handling of mail to and from many other countries.

Postage rates and zones were finally reduced to two categories: 5¢ for letters up to one-half ounce, delivered within 300 miles, and 10¢ for longer distances. To correct the abuse of "bootleg" mail, which siphoned off revenue which should have gone to the Post Office, laws were passed providing severe penalties for carrying mail and establishing private expresses on government post routes.

Notwithstanding these improvements, by 1847 the Post Office

was still unable to keep up with the growing needs of a rapidly expanding economy. It was still a collect service, with each postmaster responsible for collecting the postage due on all mail except certain periodicals, and keeping detailed records, which in turn necessitated the maintenance of a large accounting staff. Discounts were offered as inducements for prepayment of postage on newspapers and other printed matter. But there was no law which required the addressee to accept his C.O.D. mail, and there was thus no guarantee that the postal fee would be paid. For prepaid business letters (often prepaid for obvious reasons), special receipts had to be written out individually, each letter properly marked by hand, and separate records kept of such payments. This procedure was so cumbersome that postmasters in the busiest offices used special stamps known as "postmasters' provisionals" in much the same way as modern stamps are used.

Benjamin Franklin, founder of the American postal system, is portrayed on the first United States general issue stamp, the 5¢ of 1847. George Washington, who appointed the first Postmaster General under the Constitution in 1789, appears on the 10¢ value of 1847.

In 1847, all this was changed when a law was passed authorizing the sale of postage stamps for the prepayment of mail. The first stamps issued were a 5¢ stamp with an engraving of the head of Benjamin Franklin, for letters traveling less than 300 miles, and a 10¢ stamp with an engraving of George Washington from the famous Gilbert Stuart portrait.

Prepayment of postage was still not compulsory, but life was made much simpler for local postmasters—their accounts were simply charged for the stamps sent to them for sale and credited with the payments they made. In 1855, prepayment of postage became compulsory.

Meanwhile, demand was growing for greater and more economical dissemination of news and ideas, both political and cultural. In 1851, during the administration of President Millard Fillmore, the Postmaster General issued an order cutting in half the cost of carrying newspapers, if the postage were prepaid. The order also allowed for the *free* distribution of newspapers within their counties

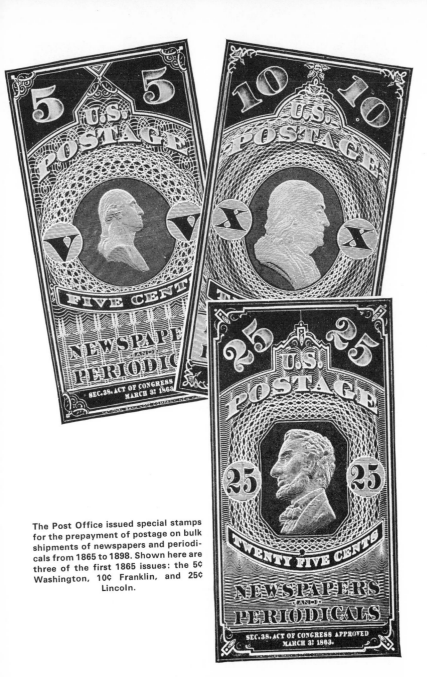

The Post Office issued special stamps for the prepayment of postage on bulk shipments of newspapers and periodicals from 1865 to 1898. Shown here are three of the first 1865 issues: the 5¢ Washington, 10¢ Franklin, and 25¢ Lincoln.

Series of 1851-56, imperforate: 1¢ dark blue Franklin; 5¢ red brown Jefferson; 10¢ green Washington; 12¢ black Washington. For the first ten years, all U.S. stamps were printed without perforations.

of origin. This led to a growth of weekly county papers which became an integral part of the development of the country as the population moved westward.

Special rates still apply to newspapers and periodicals, although a single copy today might weigh more than a whole edition one hundred years ago. This places a tremendous financial burden on the Post Office, which is constantly seeking ways to bring receipts for handling mail closer to costs. That year also, for the first time, bound books were accepted in the mail. Earlier, this had been impractical because of limited facilities for carrying the mail, but with the development of railroad and steamship mail routes, carrying bulky mail became feasible.

Prepayment of postage led to the introduction of important innovations in postal service. In 1855, registry of mail was introduced under a law providing for special handling of valuable letters and articles. The reliability and security of the registry service, though refined through the years, was essentially the same over one hundred years ago as it is today. It can best be illustrated by two classic examples.

(Left) Imperforate stamps of the 1851 issue. Imperforate pairs are much more desirable than single stamps and often cost several times as much. (Center) Beginning in 1857, stamps were issued with perforations for easier separation. (Right) Modified designs were used on the 1861 issue.

The famous "Hope Diamond" was purchased by the jeweler, Mr. Harry Winston upon the death of its owner, Mrs. Evalyn Walsh Maclean, for a sum said to exceed $1,000,000. Mr. Winston gave the jewel to the Smithsonian Institution in Washington. This priceless gem was not conveyed to Washington by armored truck, surrounded by detectives: it was simply sent by registered mail from New York— a method widely used in Europe and America for sending jewelry.

Even more spectacular was the government's transfer before World War II of more than $15,000,000,000 of gold bullion from New York and Philadelphia to Fort Knox, Kentucky, under the supervision of postal inspectors in the world's greatest movement of gold.

Series of 1857-60 perforated: 10¢ green Washington; 24¢ lilac Washington; 30¢ orange Franklin. Perforated stamps marked a real milestone in U.S. postal history. Because of the greater volume of mail, a faster method for dispensing stamps was required and machine-perforated stamps could be easily and quickly separated, instead of being cut apart by scissors.

So secure had the United States mail become that in 1858 the first postal boxes for the deposit of ordinary mail were set up in cities.

While the Post Office Department was spreading its network of routes and improving its service, the westward movement of the population, especially stimulated by the discovery of gold in California in 1848, necessitated a speeding up of communication with the western states and territories impatient for news from the east. Since the postal routes had to follow the covered wagons, and ships carrying letters, news and money still had to round Cape Horn, the service was slow and uncertain, taking weeks or months.

To meet the demand for news and mail, an enterprising transportation firm called Russell, Majors and Waddell, in April, 1860, instituted the Pony Express. This was a relay system of pony riders which carried mail and newspapers over 1,900 miles of dangerous,

These two stamps, issued in 1940 and 1960, commemorate the 80th and 100th anniversaries of the Pony Express. The fearless Pony Express riders who delivered the mail have become legends in the history of the American West.

Indian-infested terrain, through mountains and deserts, in all seasons from foul snowstorms to burning heat, from St. Joseph, Missouri, to Sacramento, California. The Pony Express required 190 thoroughly equipped relay stations, 400 attendants, and 80 hardy, resourceful, brave riders. Devoted to the service and avid for adventure, the riders were capable of enduring many hardships.

The 1,900 miles of the route, which stage coaches required weeks to cross, were traveled by the Pony Express riders in eight days in the summer and ten in the winter as they became more experienced. In March, 1861, President Lincoln's inaugural address was carried in a record seven days eleven hours. However, the Pony Express, which did much to keep California in the Union when the Southern states seceded, never received a United States contract for carrying mail, and was doomed almost before it started. Telegraph lines were already being sped out west and the transcontinental line was completed in September, 1861. One month later, the Pony Express riders delivered their last dispatches, ending a romantic and exciting period in the history of the unification of the United States.

During the Civil War, while the Union was engaged in its great

Series of 1861-66; 2¢ black Jackson; 5¢ brown Jefferson; 24¢ lilac Washington; 90¢ blue Washington. The 2¢ Jackson, an unusual specimen because the portrait covers nearly the entire stamp, is popularly known as the "Black Jack."

The Centennial of the Civil War was marked with the issuance of five stamps: 4¢ Fort Sumter, 1961; 4¢ Shiloh, 1962; 5¢ Gettysburg, 1963; 4¢ Wilderness, 1964; 5¢ Appomattox, 1965.

struggle for survival, the Post Office Department, under the able direction of Postmaster General Montgomery Blair, did not lag in its attempt to improve service, and introduced at least four important changes:

■ Up to this time, local postmasters had been *authorized* to provide home delivery service at no extra charge, but this "free" service had never been offered. Fees of 2¢ a letter and 1¢ a newspaper were charged for home delivery, in addition to the charge of 2¢ a letter collected for posting. So home service was a luxury, and people preferred to pick up the mail at their post office box.

A study of European postal systems had convinced Postmaster General Blair that the expense involved in really offering free home delivery would be more than offset by the public's increased use of postal service in general. Meanwhile, before Blair's plan was inaugurated, Joseph William Briggs, an enterprising clerk in Cleveland, developed a plan for free delivery and collection of mail and tested a trial route himself. His pioneering work was brought to Blair's attention. Blair was so impressed that he appointed Briggs to develop free city delivery throughout the country.

On July 1, 1863, delivery of mail was revolutionized when the first letter carriers distributed mail to destinations free of charge in 49 cities of the United States. At the start, local postmasters were

A railway postal clerk is shown on the 3¢ parcel post issue of 1912-13. A speeding mail train appears on the 5¢ value of the same set. The introduction of the "Railroad Post Office" in 1862 greatly improved the efficiency of mail handling.

authorized to introduce home delivery and hire carriers (at beginning salaries not to exceed $800) only if their revenues could support the service.

■ Another tremendous improvement was the introduction of the "Railroad Post Office" which greatly speeded up the handling of mail. From the time the railroads had been designated as postal routes, there had been no change in the method of handling the mail: The postal agent on board the train dropped off all mail for an area at the railroad station which served the surrounding communities. At the station the mail was sorted for redistribution to the various towns. In the towns, the mail was again sorted for local delivery. This method proved too slow, especially for commercial purposes, and there was a revival in "bootlegging" letters which required quick delivery.

Postmaster Blair set up a trial "Railroad Post Office" in 1862. This was a special Post Office car in which clerks sorted mail for each different community, leaving only local sorting for each town or village. This experiment was so successful financially and so efficient that Congress authorized the establishment of railroad post offices on all rail routes two years later.

Unfortunately, as railroad service has declined, the railroad post office has lost its importance. Hardly any first class U.S. mail travels by rail any more. Most letters travel either in giant mail trucks or by airplane.

This special 4¢ stamp, issued in 1958, marks the centennial of cross-country overland mail delivery. The overland coach carried mail and passengers from the East and Midwest to the western terminal at San Francisco. The stamp's central motif is a dramatic scene of a mail coach and horses under attack, all superimposed on a map of the Southwest.

■ During the Civil War, the Army demanded that the Post Office Department find a safe way for soldiers to send money home. Registered mail required too much paper work, and letters from soldiers containing money were too often looted. In England, the postal money order had been popular for some time, and on November 1, 1864, a similar service was started in the United States. In the six months before the war ended, over $1,000,000 of money orders were sold at fees of 10¢ for less than $20 sent, and 25¢ for larger amounts. Instead of dying out when the Army's need ended, the service became more and more popular.

Montgomery Blair, President Lincoln's Postmaster General and one of the most innovative men ever to hold the office, appears on the 15¢ 1963 airmail stamp. Blair was the principal promoter of the First International Postal Conference, forerunner of what is now the Universal Postal Union, under which the nations of the world carry one another's mail.

■ In providing such services as prepaid postage, home delivery, and postal money orders, the United States followed the lead of Europe. But the eventual formation of the Universal Postal Union came about as a result of the initiative of Postmaster General Blair. The handling of international mail had been chaotic at best. Rates varied from country to country, and often from zone to zone in individual countries. Each country handling a consignment of mail was allotted a share of the proceeds according to services claimed to have been rendered. It can easily be seen what monstrous accounting had to be kept, and how complicated international mail could get when handled in this way.

A 1949 series of three airmail stamps commemorates the 75th anniversary of the Universal Postal Union. The 10¢ value shows the Post Office Department Building in Washington, D.C.; the 15¢ pictures the world being encircled by doves in flight carrying messages; and the 25¢ depicts the world, on a dark background, with a modern four-motor plane in flight over the Pacific Ocean.

The resulting confusion was hampering the steady growth of international commerce. The first International Postal Conference was accordingly called in Paris in 1863, with 15 countries represented. Out of this and subsequent meetings grew the Postal Union, which now has over one hundred members; cooperation is so complete that there is no longer any question about the safe, expeditious and inexpensive dispatch and delivery of mail all over the world.

Toward the end of the 19th century a large portion of the population still lived in rural areas not served by home delivery. A final link in the chain of postal service was added on October 1, 1896, when the first riders of the Rural Free Delivery Service carried mail on routes in West Virginia ranging from 12 to 20 miles. In those days before the telephone and television had reached into every corner of the nation, the importance of the rural mail carrier to outlying farms could hardly be overestimated. The R.F.D. carrier might be the only bearer of news to distant farmers, carrying

A rural mail carrier at work is portrayed on this 4¢ value of the 1912-13 Parcel Post series. The beginning of Rural Free Delivery Service in 1896 helped to bind the nation closer together. Often, in those days, a family's only contact with the outside world was through the mail service.

messages regarding illness, accident, or politics. All too often he was the farmer's only contact with the outside world.

Rural free delivery has changed little in the 20th century, except to take advantage of improved roads and transportation. At first, the service was offered only where business warranted it; but after 1915 it was supplied where there were four families to a mile. In 1953 and 1958, this service was extended still further to increase the number of people covered. From its minute beginnings in 1896, Rural Free Delivery Service has grown until it now reaches almost 10,000,000 families.

In 1873, the Post Office Department issued its first postal cards, which were sold for the price of the one-cent stamp printed on it, and shortly thereafter it began to sell pre-stamped envelopes. Sales of both items have increased over the years. "Special delivery" letter service was introduced in 1885.

(Above) U.S. postal cards were introduced in 1873. The card at the top left, showing the profile of Liberty, is the original 1873 issue, with the card at the top right being the second (1875) issue. (Below) U.S. stamped envelopes were introduced in 1853.

The introduction of Special Delivery Service in 1885, and motorized Parcel Post Service in 1913 added substantially to the Post Office Department's versatility. Shown are the 30¢ Special Delivery stamp of 1954-57, and the 15¢ Parcel Post stamp of 1912-13.

On January 1, 1913, development of the motor truck made the acceptance of parcels by the mail service feasible. Packages could be sent at the sender's risk at rates per pound lower than the other classes, and insured at special rates. C.O.D. parcel post was added only seven months later.

On January 1, 1911, the Postal Savings System was started, eventually making the post office one of the larger savings banks in the country. Under the system, individuals deposited their savings with their local post offices. Interest accumulated at a lower rate than at commercial banks, but with complete safety. The post office then lent or deposited the moneys in approved national banks at interest rates great enough to cover the interest on its deposits and expenses of operation.

This service was developed to meet the needs of millions of people who had no safe place to put their small savings. (Quite a few banks had closed their doors in the financial crisis of 1907.) Commercial banks were not geared to small deposits and savings banks at that

"War Savings Certificate" stamps were issued from 1918 through 1921 to raise emergency funds for the Federal government. Priced at $4.12, they could be redeemed for $5.00 at the end of a five-year period. Albums designed for specialized U.S. collections have spaces for stamps like this.

time were concentrated in larger cities. By 1947, deposits had reached almost $3,500,000,000 dollars. But the growth of savings banks, savings and loan associations, savings departments in all kinds of banks, and Federal Deposit Insurance, have made the Postal Savings Service unnecessary. In January, 1960, the Post Office Department, in its annual report to Congress, recommended that it be abolished.

It was September, 1911, only eight years after the revolutionary flight at Kitty Hawk, North Carolina, by the Wright Brothers' airplane, that the first experiment of carrying mail by air was successfully carried out. A pilot transported a sack of mail from a tiny airfield on Long Island, New York, to the post office at Mineola, Long Island. Day after day, the plane, which was not very different from the one flown at Kitty Hawk, delivered its mail sack safely.

The postal team studying the project was so impressed that it recommended an appropriation by Congress for the initiation of an Air Mail Service. However, the plan fell through, and the experiment continued for five more years with the enthusiastic, generous and voluntary cooperation of devotees to the infant "air age."

Eventually, in 1916, $50,000 was allotted to the Post Office Department to put air mail officially on an experimental basis. However, planes could not be provided privately which met the tough requirements for continued service. The Department had to turn to the developing Air Force of the United States Army for assistance. In the spring of 1918, when the United States was gathering all its resources to help bring World War I to a victorious close, Congress appropriated $100,000 to set up a regular air mail service. On May 15, 1918, the first scheduled flights were concluded between Washington and New York.

The 24¢ value of the first airmail issue of 1918 shows the double-winged Curtiss "Jenny," a World War I training plane extensively used in those early airmail flights. The 50th anniversary of airmail service was commemorated with the 10¢ issue of 1968 showing the historic biplane.

During the early months, studies were made to determine what charges should be made for the service. Finally, air mail began to move across the continent as regular flights were started joining New York to Cleveland, then Chicago, and from there to Omaha. Finally, in September, 1919, the last gap was closed with the inauguration of a route between Omaha and San Francisco.

By 1920, air mail traveled from coast to coast in 22 hours' less time than transcontinental express trains. However, these flights could be made only in the daytime: the airfields were undeveloped and had no lights; there was no radio communication, and certainly no radar. In fact, all the pilot could do when he landed his tiny, slow biplane, with its open cockpit and no brakes, was refuel, before going on to the next stop.

All this was changed on February 22, 1921, when the Post Office arranged for its first experimental transcontinental flight involving night flying. The early relays of the flight, which started eastward from San Francisco at 4:30 that morning, were routine. But after Pilot Frank Yager arrived at North Platte in west central Nebraska at 7:48 that evening, long after dark, the rest of the trip rivaled in drama the adventures of the Pony Express riders sixty years earlier. When Jack Knight, the pilot who flew the stretch between North Platte and Omaha, was about to take off, it was noticed that the tail-skid on his plane was broken and three precious hours were lost on repairs. When Knight finally took off at 10:44 p.m. the sky was heavily overcast. Guided only by a compass and the Platte River which he saw occasionally through the clouds, he arrived two and one-half hours later at Omaha, only to find that the relays to Chicago had been cancelled because of dangerous weather conditions and that his relief pilot had left the field.

Although he was unfamiliar with the territory and had only a map to guide him, Knight decided to go on. At 2 a.m. he took off again, headed for Iowa City, which was engulfed in a heavy snowstorm. His plane was almost out of gas when he finally found the field, only to discover that it had already been closed and the crew gone home, as he was not expected. No one was there but a night watchman who heard him approaching and guided him in with a flare.

Knight and the watchman refueled the plane and he went on to Chicago, where he arrived at 8:30 in the morning, after encountering a dense fog over the Mississippi River. The rest of the flight eastward from Chicago was routine and the mail reached Hazelhurst, Long Island, New York, 33 hours and 21 minutes after it left San Francisco.

That year Congress appropriated $1,250,000 for the development of air mail and the necessary facilities, and by 1924 transcontinental air mail was on a regular 24-hour schedule. Rates were high but the savings in time were so great as to make it worth while. When the pioneering and developing stages were over, the Post Office returned to its policy of giving mail routes to private contractors, and by 1927 all air mail was carried by private contractors.

Meanwhile, international air mail had not been overlooked. On October 15, 1920, the first international air mail was carried over the 74 miles from Seattle, Washington, to Victoria, British Columbia, in Canada, in time to reach steamers sailing to or arriving from the Orient. By 1935, mail was flown on regular schedules from San Francisco to the Philippines, via Hawaii, Midway, Wake and Guam.

This special 25¢ stamp was first issued in 1935 primarily for use on mail dispatched by Trans-Pacific airmail service to and from Hawaii, Guam and the Philippines. The renowned long-range seaplane, the "China Clipper," is pictured in flight over the Pacific while a Chinese junk and modern ocean liner are shown at left and right.

In 1937 the last gap to the Asian mainland was closed with the extension of the flight to Hong Kong from the Philippines. With the development of larger and better planes, the twenties and thirties saw the opening of longer routes, and by the outbreak of World War II in 1939, all the continents were linked by air.

The speeding of air mail is not due entirely to the fact that larger and faster planes now cross the United States in less than six hours. Helicopters, too, play an important part by saving time in carrying mail between post offices and air terminals on the outskirts of the cities.

The U.S. Postal Service continues to seek ways to improve and modernize the handling of the fantastically increased volume of mail. Generally, mail is still sorted by hand, in cramped quarters,

★ ROUND ★ THE ★ WORLD ★ FLIGHT ★

AMELIA EARHART

OAKLAND
MAR 17
430PM
1937
CALIF.

UNITED STATES POSTAGE
6

HONOLULU
MAR 20
12 M
HAWAII
1937

3

AROUND ★ THE ★ WORLD
FLIGHT

Amelia Earhart
Oakland, Calif.

1937

1937

★ ROUND ★ THE ★ WORLD ★ FLIGHT ★

This historic cover, carried on the first stage of the attempted round-the-world flight by Amelia Earhart, was postmarked Oakland March 17, and Honolulu, March 20. On the latter date the plane was severely damaged and the West-to-East flight abandoned.

but the world's first "automatic post office," known as "Turnkey," was opened near Providence, R.I., with every usable mechanical and electronic device. Every post office branch now has a "zip code" or number which indicates its specific zone. This can be read by electronic scanners. Therefore, it is possible at the Rhode Island Post Office to sort, process and speed the flow of mail of all categories to all parts of the country and world.

We have all seen coin-operated stamp-vending machines, but in the Rhode Island Post Office there are machines for local users, which provide complete automatic service from weighing and stamping letters and parcels, to making change and supplying books of stamps and postcards. Machines like these have already been manufactured to be installed as unattended branch post offices in suburban areas.

Meanwhile, experiments are going forward to revolutionize mail delivery by utilizing the latest technicological developments. On June 8, 1959, a submarine in the Caribbean Sea fired a guided missile which landed under remote control at the Naval Air Auxiliary Station at Mayport, Florida. It carried not an atomic warhead, but

America's first automated post office is shown on this 4¢ commemorative. The stamp was issued at Providence, Rhode Island, on October 20, 1960, to help formally dedicate the new facility.

3,000 letters, the first of which was delivered a few hours later to President Dwight D. Eisenhower at the White House.

And now with the enormous technological developments in space and with microwaves, the Post Office is looking forward to the day when mail can be "bounced" off the moon or satellites and delivered all over the world in a matter of hours. Since 1930, photographs and facsimiles of printed matter have been transmitted by telephone, wire, and later by radio and television, but these methods are not suitable for the transmission of first class mail, whose contents must remain private. The problem of maintaining the privacy of the mail was solved when the Army made its secret research available to the Post Office Department. The Army had been experimenting with the transcontinental transmission of material. The cost of transmission in the early experiments was too high, and the number of items transmitted per minute too few to be practical. However, with the cooperation of many government agencies and private industry, in whose laboratories tests were made, the problems of high cost, slow transmission, and privacy of first class mail, were solved by 1960. Now government documents and mail are transmitted by microwave ("bounced off the moon"). Postal authorities look forward to making this latest development in communications available to the general public in the not too distant future, at costs that are little if any higher than those for handling ordinary mail.

2. Tools and Terms of Stamp Collecting

Anyone who takes stamp collecting at all seriously needs to have certain equipment. While we are concerned in this book with collecting United States stamps, you will need the same basic "tools" if you collect foreign stamps also. These are:

a stamp album
stamp tongs
stamp hinges
glassine pockets or envelopes
a perforation gauge
a watermark detector
a magnifying glass
a stamp catalogue
a stock book

To keep up a stamp collection in orderly and easily accessible form, it is necessary to keep them in an ALBUM. Here the stamps will be safe from getting lost. When you want to examine a given stamp, it will be easy to find.

An album for American stamps contains properly sized spaces with a description of the stamp that belongs in the appropriate place. The spaces are usually arranged in chronological order, with the dates of issue and the name, if it has one. The chances are that each space will contain a reproduction of the stamp that belongs there. In most cases this will be sufficient to give you guidance for putting a stamp in its proper place. In some special cases you may need to check with a catalogue before placing a stamp in the album.

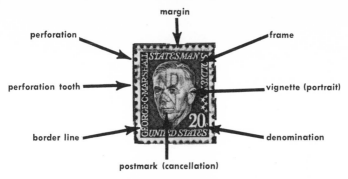

margin

perforation

frame

perforation tooth

vignette (portrait)

border line

denomination

postmark (cancellation)

Principal features of a typical stamp.

The Scott and Minkus albums can be recommended for American stamps. Scott's Minuteman Album comes in loose-leaf form and sells for $10.95. It has spaces for all the major varieties listed in Scott's Catalogue, and also provides for other types of stamps, including revenue stamps, Confederate stamps and United Nations issues. Scott Catalogue numbers are given in every case, as well as a description which specifies design, color and denomination. Annual supplements keep the album up to date.

Minkus Publications provides the All American Stamp Album, which is also loose-leaf and contains similar features and the addi-

Sample pages from an American stamp album.

tional attraction of much descriptive material dealing with the people, places and events pictured on the stamps. This album sells for $12.95.

Both these albums offer excellent value, and the choice between them will depend on individual taste.

Also available are specialized albums dealing with such items as the following:

albums for regular issues only

albums for commemorative issues only

albums for plate blocks (described on page 36)

albums for plate blocks of airmail stamps

In recent years the popularity of loose-leaf albums has increased steadily, as they have many convenient features. Not the least of these is the possibility of starting another binder when one album becomes too bulky for easy handling.

For anyone who wants to build up a fine collection, a good catalogue of American stamps is a must. Among the many virtues of such a volume is that it gives the catalogue value of every stamp, in unused and used condition. This serves as an immensely useful guide to a collector when he is buying, selling or swapping stamps.

Sample pages from American stamp catalogues.

These four stamps demonstrate four conditions: (1) VERY FINE—mint with full original gum, well centered, perforations intact, paper free of defects. (2) FINE— lightly cancelled, margins uneven, paper free of defects. (3) GOOD—heavily cancelled, off center, but no tears or bad thin spots. (4) POOR—heavily cancelled, slightly torn.

However, a catalogue must be used with some discretion. Valuations will differ somewhat from one catalogue to the next. They change from year to year, almost always going upward. Then, too, CONDITION makes a very big difference in valuation. As Scott's Catalogue puts it: "Condition is the all-important factor of price. Prices quoted are for fine specimens. Copies without gum, off center or with heavy cancellation sell for much less."

Aside from price considerations, a catalogue gives important additional information—the year of issue, the color and denomination of each stamp, as well as reproductions for easy identification.

Another valuable feature of a catalogue is that each stamp has its own identifying number. It is thus possible to talk about a stamp without needing the stamp itself or a reproduction of it. The catalogue number is enough, and this is a great help in buying and selling by mail.

The catalogue has other useful functions when used in combination with such tools as the magnifying glass and the perforation gauge, as we shall see.

The two classic works on the subject are Scott's *United States Stamp Catalogue Specialized* ($14.00) and the Minkus *New American Stamp Catalog* ($8.50). Each of these volumes has its special attractions and virtues and both should be carefully studied and compared by the prospective purchaser.

We have already had some intimation of how important condition is in determining value. This makes it essential to handle stamps carefully, so as to avoid damaging them in any way. STAMP TONGS, which are cheap as well as useful, enable the careful collector to handle his stamps without spoiling them.

The most common way of mounting stamps in an album is by using STAMP HINGES. These are made of special thin translucent paper, specially gummed on one side. Fold back one third of the hinge, exposing the gummed side. Moisten the folded third slightly and press it against the back of the stamp. The hinge should be pasted on near the top of the stamp, but not near any of the edges. Now slightly moisten the larger part of the hinge and place the stamp down in the appropriate space in the album.

Once the hinge has become thoroughly dry, the stamp can be removed at any desired time without damaging the gum on back of an unused stamp: these hinges are *peelable*.

If, however, the stamp is removed while the hinge is still moist, the gum on the back of the stamp will be irreparably damaged. And, as we have already learned, this seriously downgrades the condition of the stamp and radically reduces its value.

An increasing number of collectors are placing their thinner and more valuable stamps in glassine pockets which they mount in the album. This leaves the stamps perfectly visible without exposing them to any possible harm. Since this method of mounting has the drawback of being comparatively expensive, its use is generally limited to a collector's most prized stamps.

To make it easy to separate stamps, the government that issues stamps has holes punched in the spaces between the stamps on a sheet. This process is called perforation, and the holes are called PERFORATIONS. It is often important to be able to determine the number of perforations along the side of a stamp; this may be essential to distinguish a stamp from an identical one issued at a different time and having a different value. The only way the two stamps differ may be in the number of perforations.

To check the number of perforations we use a cardboard ruler

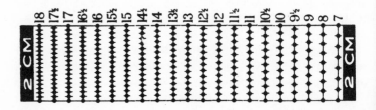

These four stamps show the same design but are differently perforated. (1) perf 12, (2) compound perforation, perf 11 x 10, (3) coil stamp, horizontal perf 8½, (4) coil stamp, vertical perf 10.

called a PERFORATION GAUGE. This cardboard ruler shows scales for all the different numbers of perforations that can be placed along a line of two centimeters (twenty millimeters). There may be as few as 7 perforations or as many as 17 along the edge. (U.S. stamps range from 8½ to 15.) By placing the stamp over the perforation gauge, you will be able to match up the right number of perforations on the scale.

If you look up a stamp in the catalogue and see the notation "Perforated $10 \times 11\frac{1}{2}$," this means that there are 10 perforations along the top and bottom, and $11\frac{1}{2}$ along the sides. Similarly, "Perf. 11 vertically" tells you that the stamp has 11 perforations at left and right. This measurement will often guide you to some startling differences in value.

A similar purpose is achieved by the use of a WATERMARK DETECTOR. Watermarks are sometimes introduced into paper in order to make counterfeiting more difficult.

The possible designs that may be used for a watermark are endless. Letters, numbers, stars, crowns are a few of the possibilities. Sometimes the design is small enough to go on a single stamp. Other times each stamp carries only a part of the watermarked design. Where you have two identical stamps, one with a watermark and one without, the two stamps may differ substantially in value. It therefore becomes important to determine which stamp has the watermark. U.S. stamps use only one watermark: USPS.

Holding up the stamp to the light will not necessarily make a watermark visible. So a small black tray is needed. Placing the stamp on a dark surface will bring out the watermark more distinctly.

Put the stamp face down on the tray. Pour a few drops of cleaning fluid on the stamp, and this will bring out the watermark design. It

With a watermark tray and fluid you can detect the watermarks in the paper on which stamps are printed.

is important to get expert advice on the choice of cleaning fluid, as some types may be dangerous to use on stamps.

After the watermark has been examined, the stamp should be placed on a clean white blotter. As the proper cleaning fluid evaporates rapidly, the stamp will dry in a few seconds, none the worse for wear.

The use of a MAGNIFYING GLASS is still another method of determining whether you have a valuable stamp. There are times when the catalogue informs you that a slight difference in the design of two stamps may result in a considerable difference in value. By scrutinizing your stamp under the magnifying glass you can tell whether you have the valuable stamp.

A STOCK BOOK is a useful adjunct to an album, especially for the purpose of keeping duplicate stamps in a readily accessible place. A stock book has cardboard pages with horizontal rows of slits for inserting stamps. The slits are small enough to hold the bottom sections of the stamps, leaving the upper sections of the stamps visible.

As we have seen, condition plays a very important role in determining the value of a stamp. It is essential to concentrate on a stamp's

Centering is all-important in determining stamp values with well centered specimens commanding premium values. Four different types of centerings are shown here: (1) No margin at the left, perforations run into the design. (2) Very small margins at top and right. (3) No margin at the right. (4) Well centered.

condition in buying as well as selling. Here are the outstanding points to be considered:

CENTERING: A stamp is said to be perfectly centered when the frame of the design is an even distance from the outer edge on all four sides. An off-center stamp is worth much less than a properly centered stamp.

PERFORATIONS: Any damage to the perforations or lack of evenness in them will lower the value of a stamp.

CANCELLATION: A used stamp is usually less valuable than an unused stamp. Even so, there are various grades of desirability in used stamps. For example, a used stamp that is only lightly cancelled is more attractive than one which is all but buried under a heavy cancellation. If, in addition, the cancellation is even in tone and concentrated in the center, it becomes still more desirable.

GUM: The finest condition of an unused stamp is *mint*—virtually in the condition in which it was issued. One of the conditions of the mint state is that the gum be in absolutely flawless condition.

DAMAGE: The presence of a tear, a crease, or thin spots on the back greatly reduces the value of a stamp.

Keeping these points in mind, a collector should always be on the alert to upgrade the condition of the stamps in his collection.

Some other definitions which the collector will find useful are the following:

ADHESIVE: Gummed stamps, as distinguished from stamps printed as part of envelopes.

AIR MAIL: Stamps that are intended to be used on mail sent by plane.

BLOCK: A set of stamps attached so as to form a square or rectangle. Blocks of four are the most common, and plate blocks are often the most popular with collectors.

CACHET: A design or illustration prepared for use on a first-day cover which is sent through the mail on the day that a new stamp is issued or some special event is celebrated.

COIL STAMPS: These are made in rolls, perforated only on two sides and straight-edged on the other two sides.

COVER: An entire envelope, including the stamp and its cancellation, which has gone through the mail.

CUT SQUARE: A stamp printed directly on the envelope (see definition of *Adhesive*) and then cut from the envelope, as a rule in a two-inch square.

DESIGN: The main pictorial image or whatever else appears within the frame of the stamp.

ENTIRE: The entire envelope, postal card or wrapper on which a stamp is printed. This is contrasted with *Cut Square*, above.

ERROR: A mistake in manufacturing a stamp. This may take the form of using the wrong color, inscription, paper or watermark, or of omitting all or part of the perforations. (See also *Invert, Perforations.*)

FACE VALUE: The denomination which appears on the stamp; the value for postal purposes. The market value—as between collectors and dealers—is determined by supply and demand.

FIRST-DAY COVER: See *Cachet* and *Cover*.

GRILL: A grid or impression embossed on the paper of a stamp. Since it is raised, it can be discovered by touching the back of the stamp or looking at it from the back.

IMPERFORATE: A stamp which has no perforations. (See *Perforations.*)

INVERT: A stamp—generally of two or more colors—a portion of which has been printed upside-down.

An 1861 patriotic Civil War cover. The letter was mailed from Baltimore to Ridgefield, Conn.

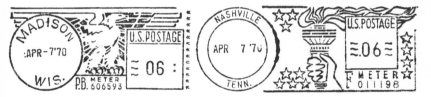

Two examples of meter stamps. Without the use of meter stamps among businesses in recent years, the Bureau of Engraving and Printing and the Post Office Department would have been overwhelmed.

The 2¢ "Black Jack" of 1861 (left) in a mint block of four with plate number. (Right) A recent plate block. Many of the early U.S. stamps were produced by private firms, like the National Bank Note Co., but after 1894 all stamps except the 1943-44 Overrun Countries series were executed by the U.S. Bureau of Engraving and Printing.

MARGIN: The space between the frame of the design on a stamp and its outer edges.

METER STAMP: This is used as a mechanical substitute for a postage stamp. The postage meter prints the amount of postage, the date and place, and in some instances a slogan or advertising material. Some collectors specialize in collecting meter cancellations.

MINT STAMP: A stamp in flawless condition, exactly as it left the printing press, is called "mint." Putting a hinge on a mint stamp changes it to an "unused" stamp.

MIXTURE: A cheap assortment of stamps sold by weight or quantity. Many of the used stamps are likely to be on the original envelope paper.

  Overprint

 Precancel

Two examples of overprints: the "Molly Pitcher" issue of 1928, and the 8¢ Franklin of 1917 overprinted for U.S. Offices in Shanghai, China. The 6¢ Roosevelt series of 1954-61 was precancelled at Philadelphia.

OVERPRINT: An addition to the stamp after its original manufacture.

PACKET: An envelope usually containing a series or set of stamps, as sold by a dealer.

PANE: A sheet of stamps, as issued. (See *Sheet*.)

PERFORATIONS: Rows of small round holes placed between the stamps on a sheet so that they can be removed without damage to any of the stamps.

PHILATELY: Stamp collecting and all that is associated with it.

PLATE NUMBER BLOCKS: When the U.S. Bureau of Engraving and Printing began producing U.S. stamps, it placed a small imprint and consecutive number in the margins of only three stamps, and collectors attempted to gather the entire series in strips of three. The block-of-six was adopted by those who favored blocks, since the margins of three stamps were required to show the full imprint and number. Soon after the introduction of rotary-press printing, the plate number was given a position in the side margin opposite the corner stamp of each pane in the full sheet. Since it was now impossible to have a block with a centrally located number, the block size was reduced to four stamps.

PRECANCELLED: A stamp that is cancelled before it is used is said to be precancelled. Such a stamp usually has two heavy horizontal bars across its face, with the place of origin stamped between the bars.

PREMIUM VALUE: The amount above face value at which a stamp may be sold.

PROVISIONAL ISSUE: Stamps issued in place of regular issues or in emergencies. The term is generally applied to the stamps issued by local postmasters before the United States began its postal issues in 1847.

ROULETTE: A method of separating stamps on a sheet by making slits in the paper, instead of by perforating.

SHEET: Usually 100 small or 50 large size stamps. Some commemoratives come in sheets of 70, jumbo stamps in sheets of 24, 32, 40, or 48.

SOUVENIR SHEETS: With stamp collectors in mind, the U.S. Postal Department issued small sheets. The margins of these sheets contain printed legends relating to the event or purpose for which the sheet was issued. (See Illus. at top of page 39.)

STRIP: Two or more stamps in a row.

SURCHARGE: An overprint which changes the face value of a stamp. This has been used on U.S. postal cards and envelopes only.

TETE-BECHE: A printing error which produces two attached stamps with one upside down in relation to the other. This has never occurred on U.S. stamps.

UNUSED STAMP: A stamp which has not been used postally but which has been hinged. (See *Mint Stamp*.)

WATERMARK: A design impressed into stamp paper during the manufacturing process, primarily as a means of guarding against counterfeiting.

3. Hobby or Investment?

It has been estimated that one tenth of all the people in the United States are stamp collectors, and that the volume of stamp business runs over $750,000,000 a year. Millions of dollars change hands in auction sales alone. The sale of commemorative stamps, first-day covers, and accessories is in the tens of millions.

Since 1910 the number of collectors has increased about 1,000 per cent, with the rate of increase steadily accelerating. Thousands of stamp dealers are needed to cater to this ever-growing demand.

As a hobby, stamp collecting has few rivals. It is comparatively inexpensive. It forms an agreeable and absorbing way of spending one's leisure time. It offers entertainment, constant novelty and the thrill of making unexpected discoveries. Oftentimes it can have a deeply educational effect; it is almost impossible to conceive, for example, that an abiding interest in commemorative stamps can fail to lead the collector in the direction of reading widely in American history, and in learning more about the great men who have played important roles in our country's development. At the very least, stamp collecting offers its devotees the means to forget the cares and irritations of their workaday lives.

United States issues may be divided conveniently into two groups, regular postal issues and commemorative issues. The first United States stamps, which appeared in 1847, came in only two denominations, the 5¢ Franklin and the 10¢ Washington stamp. The use of these men as subjects set a precedent which has been followed right into our own time. Franklin was the first Postmaster General and Washington has always been revered as the commander of the victorious Revolutionary Army and our first President. Consequently, these two men have been pictured more often on older stamps

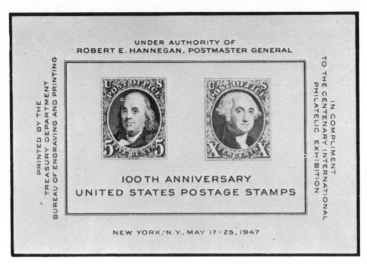

UNDER AUTHORITY OF
ROBERT E. HANNEGAN, POSTMASTER GENERAL

PRINTED BY THE
TREASURY DEPARTMENT
BUREAU OF ENGRAVING AND PRINTING

TO THE CENTENARY INTERNATIONAL
PHILATELIC EXHIBITION

IN COMPLIMENT

100TH ANNIVERSARY
UNITED STATES POSTAGE STAMPS

NEW YORK, N.Y., MAY 17-25, 1947

The first two U.S. stamps were reproduced on the souvenir sheet issued for the Centenary International Philatelic Exhibition (Cipex) held at the Grand Central Palace, New York City, in 1947.

than any other Americans. The 1847 stamps are beautifully reproduced, by the way, in the 1947 centenary souvenir sheets which can be obtained at a very moderate price.

Most United States 19th-century issues in mint or unused condition are expensive, because the supply of these stamps is comparatively small while the demand grows insatiably from year to year. However, a good many of these stamps can be obtained at quite reasonable prices in used condition, and this is probably the most practical way to build up a representative collection of these issues.

The pictorial issue of 1869. (Left) Pony Express rider, (center) early steam locomotive, (right) the steamship "Adriatic." Note the "bull's-eye" cancellation on the stamp at the left. The heavy cancellation on the stamp at the right is also typical of this period when hand-made cork cancellers were being used.

One of the most interesting early issues of regular stamps was the 1869 series. Up to that time United States stamps had featured portraits of our greatest statesmen. The 1869 series, however, was devoted to pictorial themes—a Pony Express rider, a locomotive, the landing of Columbus, signing of the Declaration of Independence, etc. Though pictorial stamps have become extremely popular in our own day, this series was unpopular. It had so little acceptance at the time that it was discontinued after a year.

A star cancellation on the 5¢ Zachary Taylor banknote stamp of 1873. Fancy cancellations add to the value of a stamp and really unusual designs like a skull and crossbones can make a stamp worth several times the value of an ordinary copy.

From the 1870's on, the growth in the volume of mail was such that the quantities of stamps issued showed a steady increase. This means, as far as present-day collectors are concerned, that the issues are more readily available at a reasonable price. One of the most interesting specialties in collecting these stamps is the quest for picturesque cancellations, such as stars, circles, etc. Some of these unusual cancellations are highly prized by specialists and result in substantial premium valuations.

A little-known case of the use of postage stamps for a non-postal purpose occurred during the Civil War. The rise in the price of metals, which started with the outbreak of the war, led people to hoard coins on such a large scale that by 1862 they had practically disappeared from circulation.

To prevent a complete paralysis of retail trade, some cities started to issue fractional paper money for small change. The use of postage stamps for this purpose became widespread. In New York City the daily volume of postage stamp purchases rose from $3,000 to

At one point during the Civil War, U.S. postage stamps encased in brass discs with mica windows were used as substitutes for small change.

$16,000. Even the Treasury Department started using postage stamps for change.

Soon a law was passed to authorize United States Assistant Treasurers to exchange postage stamps for United States currency. However, the use of the stamps was inconvenient in a number of ways. The gum made them stick to other stamps and objects. Also, the stamps quickly got soiled or torn. In some cases they were pasted on paper to be more durable.

Most of the encased postage stamps issued during the Civil War carried merchant's advertising messages on the back of the metal cases.

J. Gault, a Boston sewing-machine salesman, hit on a better idea. He designed a small brass case which left the face of the stamp visible and yet protected it from wear and damage under a transparent mica cover. This was called an "encased postage stamp." On August 12, 1862, Gault obtained a patent for making the cases. Soon various firms were purchasing the cases in order to place an advertising message on one side.

These stamps appeared in the following denominations: 1, 3, 5, 10, 12, 24, 30 and 90 cents. The top denominations, having been issued in the smallest quantities, are today the most valuable. Actually the use of these encased postage stamps lasted only about two months, after which they were replaced by the first issue of United States Fractional Currency.

One of the most important developments in United States philatelic history came with the issue of the first commemorative stamps in connection with the Columbian Exposition in Chicago in 1893, held to celebrate the 400th anniversary of the discovery of America by Columbus. The series contained no less than 16 denominations with a total face value of about $16.00. Today these stamps sell for several hundred times the face value.

The 1893 Columbian Exposition set of 16 stamps has become one of the philatelic world's most popular commemorative issues. The stamps were based on paintings and engravings by various artists and each had his own conception of what the great explorer looked like. The 1¢, for example, shows a clean-shaven Columbus in sight of land. The 2¢ shows the landing of Columbus with a full-grown beard the very next day!

From the late 1890's to 1921 there was very little variety in the regular issues, and those from 1908 to 1921 are downright monotonous, consisting in the main of countless minor variations in Franklin and Washington stamps. The slight variations are of absorbing interest to the specialist, but they offer little of interest to the general collector.

A new issue which first appeared in 1922 broke the pattern of the previous years. This was a colorful regular issue series devoted to famous Americans and pictorial stamps. It included an Indian chief, a bison, Niagara Falls, the Statue of Liberty, the Golden Gate and the Lincoln Memorial. This popular series, which continued until 1937, undoubtedly reflected the wide interest in commemorative stamps.

An American Indian chief, the Golden Gate, and the bison, as seen on the series of 1922.

This interest was further catered to with the Presidential series which started in 1938. The Presidents appeared in chronological order, with Washington on the lowest denomination and succeeding Presidents in ascending order. The commemorative influence was again seen in the Patriotic series which started in 1954. Here the emphasis was again on famous Americans and on historic shrines, such as the Alamo.

The 2¢ Liberty Bell stamp of 1926 (left) commemorates the 150th anniversary of American independence at the Sesquicentennial Exposition at Philadelphia. The 3¢ California issue of 1948 (right) marks the centennial of James W. Marshall's discovery of gold at Sutter's Mill that started the historic rush.

The primary fascination of commemorative stamps is that they build interest in important events, people and themes in our history— the landing of the Pilgrims, the Declaration of Independence, the Oregon Trail, Lincoln's Gettysburg Address, the Battle of Antietam, the invasion of Iwo Jima, the California Gold Rush, and many, many others.

Two very popular sets of commemorative stamps are the Famous American series of 1940 and the Overrun Countries issue of 1943–44. The 1940 stamps carry 35 portraits of our most distinguished authors, poets, educators, scientists, composers, artists and inventors. The 1943–44 set, very attractive in two or three colors, displays the national flags of 13 countries that were invaded and controlled by the enemy in World War II.

The U.S. Bureau of Engraving and Printing contracted with the American Bank Note Co., New York City, for the printing of the 1943-44 Overrun Countries Flags Series to take advantage of their special multicolor printing equipment.

This 1913 set of four stamps commemorates Balboa's discovery of the Pacific Ocean in 1513 and the opening of the Panama Canal in 1914. The 1¢ value portrays Balboa; the 2¢ shows the Panama Canal; the 5¢ has the Golden Gate of San Francisco Bay; and the 10¢ is the "Discovery of San Francisco Bay" taken from an oil painting.

The popularity of these stamps has made them very suitable for investment purposes. This is of course even truer of the older sets, such as the Columbian series of 1893, the Trans-Mississippi issue of 1898, the Pan-American set of 1901, the Washington series of 1932, etc. In general, the commemorative stamps of 1893 to, say, 1935 are prime investment items, as demand continues heavy while the supply is comparatively small. We shall have more to say later on about the investment aspects of collecting commemoratives.

A convenient and inexpensive way of obtaining current and recent commemorative stamps and other issues is to purchase them from the Philatelic Sales Division, U.S. Postal Service, Washington, D.C. 20265. Once the agency has your name and address, it will send you timely announcements of forthcoming issues.

The regular stream of commemorative stamps at the rate of one or two a month has created enormous interest in collecting first-day covers. These are envelopes with the new stamp affixed, postmarked with the date of issue and carrying the phrase FIRST DATE OF ISSUE stamped by the post office.

Collectors can learn about the date and place of a new issue from stamp magazines or stamp columns in newspapers. In some cases, dealers readily supply the information. In addition, the Government Printing Office periodically publishes commemorative stamp posters with photographs and descriptions of forthcoming issues. A subscription costs $3.00 a year and may be obtained from The Superintendent of Documents, Government Printing Office, Washington D.C. 20402.

Assuming that you have all the necessary information, here is how to process a first-day cover. Address an envelope to yourself. Your name and address should go in the lower part of the envelope, in order to leave room for the stamp and postmark in the upper right-hand section.

You then write to the local post office where the new stamp is being issued and ask for first-day-of-issue service. Enclose payment, which can be placed in coin cards, unless you prefer to send a money order or a certified check. One to four stamps may be requested for each envelope, and you can send as many envelopes as you wish. First-day covers may be ordered in quantity to be used as gifts or exchange items.

All this material should be enclosed in a larger envelope and sent off to the proper post office. On the day of issue, your self-addressed envelope(s) will be mailed back to you with the new stamp appropriately postmarked.

An interesting development is that a number of dealers make special "cachets" for each new stamp. These are envelopes with beautifully designed illustrations printed on the left-hand side, and make fine first-day covers.

The Project Mercury ("U.S. Man in Space") stamp is one of the most popular commemoratives issued. Whereas the average number

First Day Cover of the 4¢ Project Mercury commemorative. This is the only U.S. commemorative ever issued without advance notice. The stamps were prepared in secrecy and released only after the first American orbital flight was successfully completed.

printed in recent years has been around 130,000,000 an issue, the original print order for the Project Mercury stamp had to be increased to nearly 300,000,000 and Kennedy over 500,000,000.

Equally interesting is the fact that this was the only United States stamp prepared in complete secrecy and issued without advance notice. (The reason for this was of course the fact that the appearance of the stamp depended on the success of Astronaut John H. Glenn's flight.)

The strategic announcement of the stamp came at a time when millions of Americans were glued to their television sets after the news of Glenn's successful completion of his triple orbital flight. When the Cape Canaveral (now Cape Kennedy) post office opened the next morning, collectors were waiting in line to buy the stamp and first-day cancelled covers. At the same time, 300 post offices throughout the country had similar lines of eager customers.

The secrecy with which the whole operation was managed was amazing. The stamp went on sale on February 20, 1962, although preparations for printing had started in April, 1961. Throughout the intervening months no news of the stamp had leaked out to the public.

The die engraving and platemaking work were performed at night. Then in October, 1961, the press room was closed to all unauthorized personnel. A rumor was circulated that trial runs were being made of currency in various colors. The completed stamps were shipped in sealed packages to 301 post offices all over the country, with instructions that they were to be stored in safes and not to be opened until specific instructions were given to that effect.

A million plain envelopes were ordered for the Division of Philately and a limited number of employees worked nights and Sundays affixing singles and blocks to them. Early in November, the Post Office had completed all preparations for releasing the stamps and covers, but at this point there ensued no less than ten postponements of the flight due to unfavorable weather conditions. In the event of an unsuccessful flight the stamps would have remained in their sealed packages until completion of a successful flight.

The theory underlying investment in commemorative stamps is that they are a one-time issue, instead of being issued repeatedly like our regular stamps. As time goes on, the number of available stamps of a given commemorative issue becomes smaller and smaller, while the steady increase in the number of collectors intensifies demand.

Some sensational gains have been scored by the purchase and long-time holding of commemorative stamps, but these gains for the most part apply to the issues that appeared between 1893 and 1930. By the latter date, there were too many people in the act and commemorative issues started to be produced in such great quantities that the potential of sensational gains was severely limited.

In purchasing commemorative stamps for investment, it should be remembered that they have to be held for 10 to 15 years to show any profit. Normally it takes about three years for an issue to be used up postally. Appreciation cannot really get under way until this "dead period" is over.

The *rate* of appreciation is at its highest during the 10th to 15th year after issue. After that the annual rate of appreciation starts to drop. But many commemoratives never reach a value higher than face even after many years, for the market is highly selective.

A good example of the appreciation in the value of commemoratives is seen in the White Plains souvenir sheet of 1926. This sheet of 25 stamps (face value 50¢) was issued in a quantity of little more than 100,000—and a fair number of the stamps were used for postage. Yet ten years later the comparatively small number of sheets was selling for about $2.00. Nowadays the sheet catalogs for about $600.00 and sells for about $500.00 to $550.00.

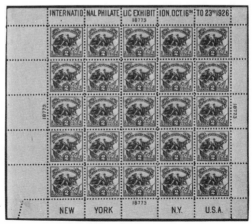

This souvenir sheet of 1926, which catalogues at about $600.00, commemorates the Battle of White Plains, N.Y., in 1776, and shows the guns commanded by Alexander Hamilton.

These stamps reduced in size.

As mentioned earlier, very few commemorative stamps issued since 1940 or thereabouts have investment value. The Pony Express stamp of 1940 is one that enjoys considerable demand, thanks to the publicity it received on issue. It all started with a statement by a noted sculptor that the express rider's horse was pictured in a physically impossible position, with three feet off the ground. The resulting heated arguments brought collectors, and non-collectors too, to the post office in search of the stamp. The resulting demand for the stamp was further stimulated by rumors that the Post Office Department would withdraw the stamp from further sale. Thus, although this commemorative was issued in a quantity of over 46,000,000, it took on and maintained a catalogue value well in excess of the valuation placed on much smaller issues.

The Three Graces from Botticelli's noted painting "Spring" are depicted on this 1940 commemorative issued to mark the 50th anniversary of the Pan-American Union.

The very next issue, the Pan-American commemorative, was issued in an even larger quantity—over 47,000,000—but this one likewise attained a good catalogue value for reasons which had nothing to do with philatelic consideration. The design shows a reproduction of Botticelli's "Three Graces," so that one might assume that the popularity of the stamp indicates delicate artistic sensibilities on the part of the public. It seems, however, that the young ladies' costumes (or lack of them) brought on rumors that the stamp might be withdrawn from circulation. This was enough to create a stepped-up demand for the stamp.

In the case of the Famous Americans series of 1940, the highest (10¢) denomination in each group naturally had the smallest issue, and just as naturally had the highest increment in value.

All of the 10¢ stamps were issued in approximately the same quantity, but the Alexander Graham Bell stamp in mint condition catalogues

The Alexander Graham Bell stamp is the most valuable of the 10-cent denominations of the 1940 Famous Americans Series.

at over $10.00, while the others in the series catalogue as low as $2.00. Shortly after the Bell stamp was released, the Bell Telephone System, now known as the American Telephone and Telegraph Co., bought up large quantities for use on parcel post packages and other mail. Since so many stamps were cancelled in the mails, the number of mint copies available to collectors is relatively small.

Going back to older issues, we find that some old covers bring amazingly high prices. In the sale of the famous Caspary collection in 1956, an envelope bearing a strip of four of the 10¢ 1847 issue brought $7,250.

One of the most interesting covers in existence is valued at over $10,000. It is from a batch of mail that was sent on the first official U.S. government airmail flight, which was made in 1859!

In that year Professor John Wise arranged to fly in his balloon *Jupiter* from Lafayette, Indiana, to New York City. This was not as fanciful as it sounds, for in 1858 he had made a flight of over 800 miles from St. Louis to Henderson, N.Y. However, Wise was forced to descend at Crawfordsville, Indiana, only 35 miles from Lafayette. The 123 pieces of mail carried by him were then re-routed to New York.

The 7¢ Balloon "Jupiter" 1959 airmail stamp features the balloon in which John Wise transported mail from Lafayette to Crawfordsville, Indiana. Of the 123 letters and 23 circulars carried on this flight, only one letter is known to exist today.

The 90¢ blue Washington issue of 1860 remains as one of the relatively few instances among U.S. stamps where a used specimen is worth more than an unused copy. Collectors should note that many of the 90¢ Washingtons have forged cancellations. Genuine cancellations on this stamp are quite rare.

Cases where a stamp is more valuable in used condition than unused are so unusual that the explanation is bound to be interesting. This is true of the 90¢ stamp issued in 1860. Supplies of this stamp were shipped to post offices only a few months before the outbreak of the Civil War.

After hostilities started, the government in Washington demanded the return of the stamps from southern post offices. The postmasters naturally ignored these demands, whereupon the federal government demonetized the issue, making it useless for postage purposes. As very few of the stamps were used, they catalogue for around $1,250.00 in used condition with a postmark that is unquestionably genuine. A cover bearing this stamp realized $10,500 in the Caspary sale. Even the unused variety catalogues for about $750.00.

Some outstanding rarities have resulted from the destruction of the remaining stock of a stamp. A notable example is the set of *Graf Zeppelin* stamps.

The famous Graf Zeppelin issue of 1930 is the most sought-after of modern U.S. stamps. Large quantities of each denomination were printed but few collectors during the depression years were able to put away extra sets because of the high $4.55 face value. The unsold copies were destroyed after a time and today the set of three stamps catalogues over $4,000.00.

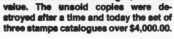

On April 19, 1930, the United States issued three stamps to be used for mail on the first Europe-to-Pan-America round trip of the *Graf Zeppelin* the following month. There were three denominations: 65¢, $1.30 and $2.60. The *Graf Zeppelin* was a German dirigible, built and commanded by Dr. Hugo Eckener. On this flight the stages covered were Germany-Spain-Brazil-United States-Spain-Germany.

Although the *Zeppelin* stamps were destined to become quite valuable because of the small issue, stamp collectors showed very little interest in them. After all, the sum of $4.55 needed for the three stamps was a considerable amount in those days of the Depression.

After some 65,000 sets had been purchased by collectors, the Post Office destroyed the remaining stamps on June 30, 1930. Ninety per cent of the issue disappeared in this way.

The scarcity value of the *Zeppelin* stamps has since mounted year by year. Here are the approximate catalogue values at which they have been quoted in recent years, in unused condition:

	single stamps	block of 4	sheet of 50
65¢	$750.00	$3,000.00	$37,500.00
1.30	1,500.00	6,000.00	75,000.00
2.60	2,000.00	8,000.00	100,000.00

In 1933, the *Graf Zeppelin* made a "Century of Progress" flight from Miami to Akron to Chicago and then to Europe. On this occasion, a 50¢ stamp was issued in connection with the flight. We might expect that by this time collectors had learned their lesson. But this new stamp likewise went begging—perhaps because the Depression had deepened. At any rate, after an interval of several years the Post Office destroyed the existing stock of the new stamp.

While its rise has not been so sensational as in the case of the 1930 stamps, the appreciation has been quite substantial, with single

Issued for use on airmail matter carried on the flight of the Graf Zeppelin to the Century of Progress Exposition in Chicago in October, 1933, this 50¢ stamp has steadily risen in value. To the right is the airship's main hangar at Friedrichshafen, Germany, and left is Chicago's Federal Building.

specimens quoted at $175.00, a block of four at $700.00 and a sheet. of 50 in the neighborhood of $8,500.00.

Color errors have also been a notable source of spectacular values. In this field an outstanding rarity is the 4-cent stamp of the Columbian (1893) series, printed blue instead of ultramarine. In a 1962 auction sale a plate number strip of four of these stamps sold for $5,000. This is a high value to place on a "shade of difference."

But the most sensational errors of all have turned up in "inverts," where a stamp is printed in several colors and run through the press separately for each color, with the occasional and unintentional result that one section is printed upside down.

No less than three denominations of the 1869 issue are known to exist with inverted centers. This applies to the 15¢, 24¢ and 30¢ denominations. The story goes that a man named Anthony, who was a government agent for the sale of postage and revenue stamps,

The first U.S. invert errors occurred with the issuance of the country's first pictorial series in 1869. The bi-colored 15¢, 24¢ and 30¢ values in this issue have inverted centers.

This stamp enlarged.

noticed that he had a sheet of the 15¢ stamps with inverted centers. One stamp had already been sold, but, displaying commendable honesty (and ignorance of philately), Mr. Anthony returned the remaining stamps to Washington and requested a sheet of normal stamps in return.

When the news of Anthony's discovery spread among stamp collectors, they began a vigorous search which led to the discovery of other 15¢ and 24¢ stamps with inverted centers. As for the 30¢ inverts, they did not turn up until several years later. The approximate catalogue values of the three inverts are as follows:

	Unused	Used
15¢	$75,000.00	$10,000.00
24¢	62,500.00	10,000.00
30¢	70,000.00	27,500.00

Some 1¢, 2¢ and 4¢ values in the 1901 bi-colored
Pan-American series were printed by error with
inverted centers. These stamps are highly prized
collectors' items today.

These stamps enlarged

Three denominations of the Pan-American series of 1901 turned
up with inverted centers: 1¢, 2¢ and 4¢. In Brooklyn, a man who was
not a stamp collector purchased ten 2¢ stamps. Surprising as it
sounds, he used four of the stamps for postage before noticing that
the centers were inverted. Then he wrote to the Bureau of Printing
and Engraving in Washington to inquire whether these stamps could
be used for postage. However, before receiving a reply he learned
how valuable his find was, and sold the remaining stamps to a
collector at a handsome profit. There are thought to be a thousand
of the 1¢ inverts in existence, and specimens have been found as
far apart as Connecticut and Alabama. About 160 of the 2¢ inverts
are known to exist. In the case of the 4¢ invert, a little over 200 are
thought to be in existence. The catalogue values are approximately
as follows:

	Unused	Used
1¢	$7,000.00	$2,000.00
2¢	32,500.00	8,500.00
4¢	10,000.00	—

The last place in the world where one would dream of buying a
rare stamp is the post office; but it has happened in the past, and will
doubtless happen again.

In 1918, when airplane transport of mail was just getting under
way, the government set up airmail routes between New York,
Philadelphia and Washington. For this occasion a special 24¢ stamp
was issued to cover the cost of airmail and special delivery.

To do justice to the occasion the stamp was printed in two colors. This meant that the sheets had to be run through the press twice— once for the frame in red, and then for the 1918-type plane in blue.

Before the second run could be started, the sheets had to be left to dry. During one of these pauses a sheet was dropped and accidentally turned around when repiled to be fed back into the press. The result was of course that the center of the stamp (with the airplane) was printed upside down. The mistake was not caught by the printers or the inspectors. Eventually the erroneously printed sheet was included in the regular stock of normal sheets of the stamp, which went on sale the following week.

In Washington, a Mr. William Robey went to the post office to buy a sheet of 100 of the new stamps to use on first-day covers he intended to mail to friends in Philadelphia and New York.

The 24¢ 1918 airmail invert is regarded as the rarest of all U.S. stamps. Only a single sheet of these stamps was erroneously printed and issued with the airplane upside down. A single copy of one of these stamps is now valued well in excess of $125,000. Blocks of four are valued at $500,000.

This stamp enlarged.

Being a stamp collector, Mr. Robey immediately noticed the upside-down planes and realized that he had acquired a treasure for $24.00. Imprudently, but understandably, he asked the post office clerk if he had any more stamps with the plane upside down. The clerk, now aware that he should never have parted with the stamps, asked to have them back. But Mr. Robey refused, and later, when postal inspectors insisted on the return of the stamps, he refused to hand them over on the grounds that they were his legal property.

Shortly thereafter he sold the sheet of 100 stamps in Philadelphia to the purchasing agent for Colonel Edward H. R. Green, perhaps the most famous, and certainly the wealthiest, collector of his time. In a few days, the agent resold the stamps to the Colonel for $20,000.

After Green's death in 1936 a plate block was sold from the sheet at an auction. The four stamps alone brought $27,000. Today, single copies of the invert are valued at over $125,000, and blocks of four at $500,000.

In 1962, some 44 years after the appearance of the airmail invert, another invert turned up. This was in connection with the commemorative issued in honor of Dag Hammarskjold, the late Secretary General of the United Nations.

The stamp was printed in yellow, brown and black. Such multicolored stamps are usually turned out on a Giori press, which does the whole job in one operation with no possibility of error. In this case, however, the stamp was produced on a single-color conventional press, which meant passing it through the press once for each color.

Somehow several sheets which had received the black frame imprint were negligently fed back into the press upside down. The result was that the yellow vignette containing the denomination,

The U.S. Dag Hammarskjold memorial stamp of 1962 received worldwide publicity because of an unusual color error. (Left) Yellow color plate inverted. Note the color in left and right margins, and white area around building. (Right) Normal stamp.

which should normally have appeared at the lower left, turned up at the upper right, in an inverted position.

Apparently this happened to 400 stamps in all, out of an issue of 120,000,000 stamps. The lucky collectors in Irvington, N.J., Cuyahoga Falls, Ohio, and Carmel, N.Y., who hit on the error sheets thought they had struck it rich; but they were in for a cruel disappointment.

On learning of the errors the Post Office Department immediately took steps to carry out its "policy of avoiding production of rare or overvalued philatelic items." The department was concerned, it explained, lest an "artificially inflated value might be given these few stamps."

To destroy the value of the inverts, the Post Office immediately printed up an additional 40,270,000 imperfect stamps identical with the original (and unintentional!) errors. This surprising development aroused a lively controversy over the propriety of the action taken by the government. Still, it would be premature to conclude that the day of great rarities has come to an end.

The liberal use of color on stamps was the dominant element of the U.S. philatelic scene in the 1960's as the Post Office Department finally departed from its conservative design policies. The new Giori presses made it possible to produce multicolored stamps quickly and inexpensively.

As part of its commemorative program, the Post Office regularly began issuing stamps in full color showing paintings and engravings by American artists. Those represented on stamps of the 1960's include Frederic Remington, Winslow Homer, John James Audubon, Stuart Davis, Charles M. Russell, John Singleton Copley, Mary Cassatt, Thomas Eakins, John Trumbull, and Grandma

This 1962 multicolored stamp showing Winslow Homer's famous painting "Breezing Up" is part of the American Artists series.

Moses. In fact, art stamps have become highly popular with collectors the world over, as many countries now issue them in great variety.

The first special Christmas stamp was issued in 1962 and a new design has been produced annually for the holiday season ever since. In recent years, the Christmas stamps have featured works of religious art. These stamps, which are placed on general sale from early November through December 31, now have press runs of well over a billion copies each.

The Christmas stamps of 1964 were a high point in stamp design. For the first time in U.S. philatelic history, four different stamps were printed on the same sheet. Through the use of the modern Giori presses, the red and green stamps on white paper were produced in panes of 100, each containing 25 blocks of the four different stamps. Fittingly enough, on the first day of issue (November 9, 1964), these

Christmas stamps were placed on sale at Bethlehem, Pennsylvania.

Another philatelic milestone was reached in 1968 when the Post Office produced the Historic Flags set of ten stamps on a single pane of 50. The ten varieties were printed vertically in rows of 10 so that the same design appears horizontally in rows of five. A plate strip of 20 stamps, with two of each variety, is required to have all the stamps in plate block form.

The Beautification of America issue of 1969 marked the second time that four different stamps were printed on the same sheet, and the first time that four designs appeared on a single pane of 50. Collectors and dealers everywhere hailed this set as one of the most attractive ever produced by the United States. Later in 1969, the XI International Botanical Congress issue, also consisting of four designs printed on a single pane of 50, made its appearance. These stamps, too, received immediate and wide acceptance among philatelists because of their attractiveness.

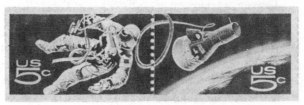

The "twin" stamps of 1967 depict the space walk that was successfully accomplished during Project Gemini.

The Post Office also produced a set of "twin" stamps, an issue which saluted the nation's accomplishments in space. First-day ceremonies were held at Kennedy Space Center, Florida, on September 29, 1967. An astronaut walking in space is seen at the left, while the Gemini 4 spacecraft and the earth are seen at the right, with the twin stamps separated by perforations only. While the twin stamps were designed to hail the U.S. space program in general, they specifically refer to the Gemini IV flight of June 3–7, 1965, in which Major Edward H. White became the first American to walk in space. The Mission commander was Major James A. McDivitt.

Throughout the 1960's, space stamps were issued by many countries in great variety.

The U.S. Post Office continued its efforts to effect a more imaginative stamp program when, in 1969, it released the first three "Jumbo" stamps: a Moon Landing commemorative on September 9; an

DWIGHT D. EISENHOWER

(Above) An astronaut stepping on the lunar surface is portrayed on this jumbo-sized 10 cent airmail stamp issued to celebrate the successful Apollo 11 mission of July 20, 1969.

(Right) A newspaper photographer caught President Eisenhower's "trademark" grin on a 1963 photo, and it was used for this 1969 memorial issue, another jumbo-sized stamp.

Eisenhower portrait on October 14; and a William M. Harnett—American Art stamp on December 3. These were the largest U.S. postage stamps ever issued, measuring $1\frac{1}{4}$ by 2 inches as opposed to the .84 by 1.44 inches for the regular commemoratives.

The "first landing on the moon stamp" is interesting not only because it records the July 20, 1969, space epic by showing an astronaut on the lunar surface. What is most exciting is that the plates used for printing the stamp were made from a master steel die that had been on board the Apollo 11 landing module, and had made the round-trip journey to the moon!

Immediately after the moon landing commemorative was issued, the Post Office Department was deluged with first-day cancellation requests and it took nearly five months to complete the staggering job. Postmaster-General Winton M. Blount reported that a record 8,743,070 first-day cancellations were applied to covers bearing the jumbo 10¢ airmail stamp. This was nearly three times greater than the previous first-day cover record of approximately 3 million for the 4¢ Project Mercury stamp issued in February, 1962.

The commemorative stamp honoring President Eisenhower is based on a photograph of the late chief executive taken in 1963 at his Gettysburg, Pennsylvania, farm by *Cleveland Press* photographer Bernard Noble. The photo features the Eisenhower "trademark" grin.

U.S. 6c AMERICAN BALD EAGLE

U.S. 6c AFRICAN ELEPHANT HERD

U.S. 6c HAIDA CEREMONIAL CANOE

U.S. 6c THE AGE OF REPTILES

Three of the stamps in the "Natural History" series of 1970 have designs based on exhibits which can be seen at the American Museum of Natural History in New York City: the African elephant herd in the Carl Akeley Hall, the American Bald Eagle, and the ceremonial canoe of the Haida Indians. The theme for the fourth stamp has been adapted from a mural, The Age of Reptiles, at the Peabody Museum of Yale University.

The still life entitled "Old Models," by William M. Harnett (1848–92) reproduced on the third Jumbo stamp, is also the ninth stamp in the annual American Paintings series. The original Harnett painting hangs in Boston's Museum of Fine Arts.

The 1969 Christmas stamp, "Winter Sunday in Norway, Maine," measuring 1 by 1¾ inches, is also larger than the regular-size commemoratives.

When the set of four "Natural History" stamps was released on May 6, 1970, it marked the first time in U.S. postal history that four jumbo-sized stamps were issued simultaneously and as a block. The set was issued to commemorate the 100th anniversary of the founding of the American Museum of Natural History in New York City.

On August 2, 1971 it issued its second twin stamp to commemorate a Decade of Space Achievement. As in the issue of 1967, each stamp is complete by itself, but together they make one design depicting Earth orbiting the moon on which a landing craft is seen in the background with the Astronauts in their Lunar Rover in the fore-ground. The first day of issue was celebrated at Kennedy Space Center, Florida; Houston, Texas; and the George C. Marshall Space Flight Center in Huntsville, Alabama.

Astronauts David R. Scott and James B. Irwin established the first post office on the moon when they cancelled the first letter there. The cancellation reads, "United States on the Moon, August 2, 1971." The envelope, a stamp pad, and a rubber post-marking device were in a container made of beta cloth, a material which can withstand a temperature of 2400°, attached under the driver's seat of the Lunar Rover.

The Postal Service Employees issue of April 30, 1972 introduced another innovation. Honoring the postal workers, it consists of 10 individual subjects printed in horizontal rows of ten in panes of 50. For the first time in postal history, each stamp bears a descriptive message printed under the adhesive on the reverse.

The Cape Hatteras Commemorative issue of 1972 in the National Parks Centennial series, was the first U.S. block of four 2¢ stamps to form a single square design, although each stamp in the set is complete in itself. Other stamps in the issue are Wolf Trap Farm, Virginia, Old Faithful, Yellowstone, and Mt. McKinley, Alaska.

On November 15, 1974 the Christmas Stamp depicting the Dove of Peace Weathervane atop Mount Vernon was the first *self-adhesive* stamp ever to be issued. Released only as a precancelled stamp to test such precancellation to speed up seasonal mail, it was sold only through the post offices in the test areas—Allegheny, Chicago, Salt Lake City and Tampa.

U.S. BICENTENNIAL SERIES

On July 4, 1971 the U.S. Postal Service inaugurated its series of stamps commemorating the Bicentennial of the American Revolution with the release of a stamp depicting the emblem of the Bicentennial Commission. Each year since then it has issued stamps either singly or in blocks of four with the Bicentennial emblem and inscription either on the stamp or in the block margin.

The block of four stamps commemorating the Boston Tea Party, issued on July 4, 1973, is a notable example of four self-contained stamps making a single design as a set. It depicts the scene in Boston

Harbor in 1773 when colonists, protesting objectionable taxes, dumped chests of tea into the harbor.

A stamp based on John Trumbull's famous painting was released on June 17, 1975 to commemorate the Battle of Bunker Hill. Only the left portion of the painting was used. The right portion appeared in a 6¢ stamp in the American Painting Series of 1968.

Bicentennial issues continued to be produced in a myriad of varieties. On Jan. 1, 1976, a strip of three, depicting Archibald M. Willard's noted painting "The Spirit of '76," was released.

Then on Feb. 23, the U.S. Postal Service came out with a magnificent sheet of fifty 13¢ values, portraying all the state flags in the order of the respective states' admission to the Union, from Delaware to Hawaii. This marked a milestone in U.S. philatelic history since never before had a single sheet consisted of fifty different designs.

At Philadelphia's International Philatelic Exhibition ("Interphil '76"), the U.S. released four large souvenir sheets, with each sheet showing details from renowned paintings depicting events of the Revolutionary era.

A strip of four 13¢ stamps, featuring a reproduction of John Trumbull's painting "Declaration of Independence," made its appearance, appropriately enough, on July 4, 1976.

Bicentennial stamps kept rolling off the presses, with many of the post-July 4, 1976 issues commemorating various events of the Revolutionary War. For example, the Oct. 7, 1977, 13¢ specimen marks the 200th anniversary of Burgoyne's defeat at Saratoga.

The U.S. Postal Service has proceeded more actively than ever in issuing truly attractive multicolored stamps. A large number are produced in "se-tenant" blocks of four. (The term se-tenant refers to any group of stamps in which there are at least two designs in unseparated condition.)

Many of the se-tenant blocks of four deal with specific aspects of Americana, including: "Pueblo Indian Pottery" (1977); "Skilled Hands for Independence" (1977); "American Quilts" (1978); "American Dance" (1978); and "Pennsylvania Toleware" (1979).

UNITED STATES POSTAGE STAMPS

1847

		unused	used
5¢	Franklin—Red brown, no perforations	$1,500.00	$450.00
10¢	Washington—Black, no perforations	10,000.00	1,000.00

1851-56

1¢	Franklin—Blue, no perforations	$175.00	$40.00
3¢	Washington—Pale red, no perforations	50.00	4.00
5¢	Jefferson—Red brown, no perforations	3,000.00	400.00
10¢	Washington—Green, no perforations	600.00	125.00
12¢	Washington—Black, no perforations	650.00	125.00

1857-60

1¢	Franklin—Blue, perforated	$300.00	$150.00
3¢	Washington—Pale red, perforated	25.00	3.00
5¢	Jefferson—Red brown, perforated	225.00	75.00
10¢	Washington—Green, perforated, Roman numerals	75.00	25.00
12¢	Washington—Black, perforated	125.00	35.00
24¢	Washington—Lilac, perforated	300.00	100.00
30¢	Franklin—Orange, perforated	350.00	150.00
90¢	Washington—Blue, perforated	750.00	1,250.00

1861-66†

1¢ Franklin—Blue, smaller portrait	$60.00	$10.00
2¢ Jackson—Black	62.50	12.50
3¢ Washington—Rose, large portrait	20.00	1.00
5¢ Jefferson—Buff or yellow	1,000.00	100.00
5¢ Jefferson—Brown	350.00	37.50
10¢ Washington—Green, "10"	85.00	10.00
12¢ Washington—Black, "12"	175.00	20.00
15¢ Lincoln—Black	275.00	30.00
24¢ Washington—Lilac, "24"	300.00	30.00
30¢ Franklin—Orange, "30"	225.00	27.50
90¢ Washington—Blue, "90"	625.00	100.00

1¢ Franklin—Blue, grilled	100.00	25.00
2¢ Jackson—Black, grilled	55.00	10.00
3¢ Washington—Red, grilled	32.50	1.75
5¢ Jefferson—Brown, grilled	375.00	100.00
10¢ Washington—Green, grilled	200.00	27.50
12¢ Washington—Black, grilled	225.00	32.50
15¢ Lincoln—Black, grilled	225.00	37.50
24¢ Washington—Gray, grilled	575.00	150.00
30¢ Franklin—Orange, grilled	625.00	125.00
90¢ Washington—Blue, grilled	1,250.00	375.00

† Stamps 1867-71 have grill embossed in paper (see page 34).

1869

1¢ Franklin—Buff		$55.00	$17.50
2¢ Rider on Horse—Brown		30.00	7.50
3¢ Locomotive—Blue		17.50	1.75
6¢ Washington—Light blue		100.00	20.00
10¢ Eagle on Shield—Yellow		110.00	17.50
12¢ Ship—Green		100.00	17.50
15¢ Landing of Columbus—Brown and blue		125.00	20.00
24¢ Declaration of Independence—Green and violet		300.00	75.00
30¢ Eagle on Shield and Flags—Blue and red		350.00	50.00
90¢ Lincoln—Red and black		850.00	250.00

1870-71

1¢ Franklin—Light blue, grilled		$100.00	$12.50
2¢ Jackson—Brown, grilled		55.00	7.50
3¢ Washington—Green, grilled		40.00	1.75
6¢ Lincoln—Red, grilled		200.00	35.00
7¢ Stanton—Vermilion, grilled		175.00	35.00

10¢ Jefferson—Brown, grilled	750.00	200.00
12¢ Henry Clay—Dull violet, grilled	8,000.00	900.00
15¢ Webster—Orange, grilled.....................	675.00	325.00
24¢ Gen. Scott—Purple, grilled	unknown	7,500.00
30¢ Alexander Hamilton—Black, grilled	2,000.00	575.00
90¢ Comm. Perry—Carmine, grilled	3,000.00	350.00

1873-88

1¢ Franklin—Blue	$65.00	$2.50
2¢ Jackson—Brown	55.00	2.50
2¢ Jackson—Vermilion	25.00	1.75
3¢ Washington—Green	10.00	.20
3¢ Washington—Vermilion	20.00	17.50
5¢ Zachary Taylor—Blue	65.00	3.75
6¢ Lincoln—Pink or red	225.00	5.00
7¢ Stanton—Vermilion	150.00	20.00
10¢ Jefferson—Brown	80.00	5.00
12¢ Henry Clay—Dull violet	250.00	17.50
15¢ Webster—Vermilion	55.00	6.75
24¢ Gen. Scott—Purple.........................	235.00	30.00
30¢ Alexander Hamilton—Black	185.00	10.00
30¢ Alexander Hamilton—Orange brown	175.00	37.50
90¢ Comm. Perry—Carmine.....................	500.00	50.00
90¢ Comm. Perry—Purple	425.00	75.00

1881-87

1¢ Franklin—Blue, same size stamp, small bust	$25.00	$ .35
2¢ Washington—Brown.........................	8.50	.08
2¢ Washington—Green	7.50	.05
4¢ Jackson—Green	57.50	3.25
4¢ Jackson—Red	50.00	5.75
5¢ Garfield—Brown............................	45.00	2.25
5¢ Garfield—Blue	37.50	2.50

1890-93

1¢	Franklin—Blue. (This series without triangles)	$8.75	$.10
2¢	Washington—Deep red........................	7.50	.05
3¢	Jackson—Purple	32.50	1.75
4¢	Lincoln—Dark brown........................	35.00	1.00
5¢	Grant—Chocolate	35.00	.90
6¢	Garfield—Red brown	30.00	6.25
8¢	William T. Sherman—Lilac....................	18.75	3.75
10¢	Daniel Webster—Green	57.50	1.00
15¢	Henry Clay—Deep blue	75.00	9.00
30¢	Jefferson—Black............................	100.00	10.00
90¢	Comm. Perry—Orange	215.00	45.00

1893

Columbian Exposition Issue

449,195,550	1¢ Columbus Sighting Land—Blue.....	$20.00	$.35
1,464,588,750	2¢ Columbus Landing—Violet	18.00	.07
11,501,250	3¢ "Santa Maria"—Green	50.00	12.00
19,181,550	4¢ Fleet of Columbus—Blue	60.00	4.00
35,248,250	5¢ Columbus Asking Aid of Isabella—Chocolate	65.00	4.50
4,707,550	6¢ Columbus at Barcelona—Purple	65.00	12.00
10,656,550	8¢ Columbus Restored to Favor—Magenta.....................	50.00	6.00
16,516,950	10¢ Columbus Presents Natives—Gray black........................	85.00	4.50
1,576,950	15¢ Columbus Announces his Discovery—Green	150.00	45.00
617,250	30¢ Columbus at La Rabida—Orange brown	200.00	65.00
243,750	50¢ Recall of Columbus—Slate	300.00	100.00
55,050	$1 Queen Isabella Pledges her Jewels—Salmon	1,000.00	350.00

45,550 $2 Columbus in Chains—Brown red ... 1,100.00   325.00
27,650 $3 Columbus Tells of his 3rd Trip—Green 1,650.00   600.00
26,350 $4 Queen Isabella and Columbus—Red . 2,750.00   850.00
27,350 $5 Bust of Columbus—Black 3,000.00 1,000.00

1894-1898—REGULAR ISSUES

Regular Issues

1¢ Franklin—Light blue (This series with triangles)	$12.50	$2.50
1¢ Franklin—Dark blue	17.50	1.00
1¢ Franklin—Green	3.75	.06
2¢ Washington—Carmine	1.75	.06
3¢ Jackson—Purple	10.00	.55
4¢ Lincoln—Brown	12.50	.55
5¢ Grant—Chocolate	10.00	1.00
5¢ Grant—Blue	8.75	.40
6¢ Garfield—Brown or dark brown	25.00	2.00
8¢ Sherman—Violet brown	10.00	.55
10¢ Webster—Green	22.50	.75
10¢ Webster—Orange brown	50.00	1.00
15¢ Henry Clay—Blue	90.00	4.50
15¢ Henry Clay—Olive green	60.00	3.75
50¢ Jefferson—Orange	125.00	10.00
$1 Comm. Perry—Black	350.00	30.00
$2 James Madison—Blue	575.00	150.00
$5 John Marshall—Dark green	1,200.00	125.00

Blocks of 4, both used and unused, of these and subsequent issues are worth 4 times the listed price.

1898

Trans-Mississippi Issue

70,993,400	1¢ Marquette on the Mississippi—Green	$22.50	$4.00
159,720,800	2¢ Farming in the West—Copper	20.00	1.00
4,924,500	4¢ Indian Hunting Buffalo—Orange ....·	90.00	15.00
7,694,180	5¢ Fremont on the Rocky Mountains— Blue	90.00	12.50
2,927,200	8¢ Troops Guarding Train—Brown	125.00	25.00
4,629,760	10¢ Hardships of the Trip—Violet	125.00	12.50
530,400	50¢ Prospector—Green	500.00	80.00
56,900	$1 Cattle in Storm—Black............	1,000.00	400.00
56,200	$2 Mississippi River Bridge—Orange brown	1,500.00	550.00

1901

Pan-American Exposition Issue (see Illus. p. 53):

91,401,500	1¢ Steamboat—Green and black	$20.00	$3.75
	Same—Inverted center	6,250.00	2,000.00
209,759,700	2¢ Train—Red and black.............	20.00	.85
	Same—Inverted center	32,500.00	8,500.00

5,737,100	4¢	Automobile—Brown and black	95.00	15.00
		Same—Inverted center 10,000.00		
77,201,300	5¢	Bridge at Niagara Falls—Blue and black	95.00	15.00
4,921,700	8¢	Canal Locks—Brown violet and black	125.00	37.50
5,043,700	10¢	Ocean Liner—Yellow brown and black	135.00	17.50

1902-3 REGULAR ISSUES

1¢	Franklin—Green	$4.75	$ .05
2¢	Washington—Red (flags at sides)	4.50	.05
2¢	Washington—Red (shields at sides)	3.75	.05
3¢	Jackson—Purple	22.50	1.50
4¢	Grant—Brown.............................	22.50	.75
5¢	Lincoln—Blue.............................	22.50	.75
6¢	Garfield—Claret	27.50	1.50
8¢	Martha Washington—Lavender	20.00	1.00
10¢	Webster—Red brown	35.00	.75

13¢ Benjamin Harrison—Deep Violet	18.50	6.50
15¢ Henry Clay—Olive green	95.00	4.25
50¢ Jefferson—Orange	285.00	20.00
$1 David Farragut—Black	475.00	30.00
$2 Madison—Very deep blue	625.00	135.00
$5 Marshall—Very dark green	1,375.00	425.00

1906-08

1¢ Franklin—Green. (This series without perforations)	$22.50	$12.75
2¢ Washington—Red	20.00	12.00
5¢ Lincoln—Blue	425.00	250.00

1904

Louisiana Purchase Issue

79,779,200	1¢ Livingston—Green	$22.60	$4.25
192,732,400	2¢ Jefferson—Carmine	17.50	1.00
4,544,600	3¢ James Monroe—Violet	62.50	22.50
6,926,700	5¢ William McKinley—Blue	80.00	15.00
4,011,200	10¢ Map of Louisiana Purchase—Brown	150.00	22.50

1907

Jamestown Exposition Issue

77,728,794	1¢ Capt. John Smith—Green	$17.50	$4.50
149,497,994	2¢ Founding of Jamestown—Carmine	17.50	3.00
7,980,594	5¢ Pocahontas—Blue	100.00	20.00

1908-21—REGULAR ISSUES

1¢	Franklin—Green, *One cent*	$4.25	$ .06
1¢	Washington—Green	3.75	.06
2¢	Washington—Carmine, *Two cents*	4.00	.06
2¢	Washington—Carmine	4.00	.06
3¢	Washington—Violet	4.25	.10
4¢	Washington—Brown	6.75	.10
5¢	Washington—Blue	2.25	.08
5¢	Washington—Carmine red (an error)	375.00	200.00
6¢	Washington—Orange	5.00	.11
7¢	Washington—Black	12.50	.65

8¢ Washington—Olive green	13.75	1.50
8¢ Franklin—Olive green	4.25	.35
9¢ Franklin—Light red	10.50	1.50
10¢ Washington—Yellow	25.00	.60
10¢ Franklin—Yellow	7.50	.10
11¢ Franklin—Green	7.50	2.25
12¢ Franklin—Dark brown	5.25	.25
13¢ Washington—Green	17.50	12.50
13¢ Franklin—Light green	6.75	4.75
15¢ Washington—Blue	25.00	3.00
15¢ Franklin—Gray	15.00	.60
20¢ Franklin—Blue	12.75	.20
30¢ Franklin—Orange	12.75	.60
50¢ Washington—Violet	135.00	7.50
50¢ Franklin—Violet	17.50	.35
$1 Washington—Violet brown	250.00	35.00

$1 Franklin—Violet brown	75.00	.75
$2 Madison—Blue, wide perfs.	275.00	20.00
$2 Franklin—Orange and black	725.00	115.00
$2 Franklin—Red and black	250.00	17.50
$5 John Marshall—Light green	275.00	20.00
$5 Franklin—Green and black	275.00	17.50

1909

148,387,191	2¢ Lincoln, Memorial Issue—Carmine ..	$5.75	$2.50
1,273,900	Same—Without perforations, wide margins around entire stamp	35.00	15.00
637,000	Same—Printed on gray paper (compared to the regular paper, this stamp has a dark gray almost blue background)	200.00	90.00

152,887,311	2¢ William H. Seward, Alaska-Yukon Pacific Issue—Carmine	8.50	2.00
525,400	Same—Without perforations, wide margins around entire stamp	45.00	12.50
72,634,631	2¢ "S.S. Clermont" and "S.S. Half-Moon," Hudson-Fulton Celebration—Carmine	8.50	2.50
216,480	Same—Without perforations, wide margins around entire stamp	50.00	15.00

1912-13

Panama-Pacific Issue (see Illus. p. 44)

334,796,626	1¢ Balboa—Green	$17.50	$1.50
503,713,086	2¢ Panama Canal Locks—Red	17.50	.50
29,088,726	5¢ Golden Gate—Blue	60.00	7.50
16,968,365	10¢ Discovery of San Francisco Bay—Orange	120.00	15.00
	Same—Yellow	95.00	16.50

1919

99,585,200	3¢ Figure of Victory, End of World War I—Violet	$8.75	$3.25

1920

Pilgrim Tercentenary Issue

137,978,207	1¢ "Mayflower"—Green	$5.75	$2.25
196,037,327	2¢ Pilgrims Landing—Red	8.50	1.75
11,321,607	5¢ Pilgrims Compact—Blue	42.50	15.00

1922-1938—REGULAR ISSUES

½¢ Nathan Hale—Brown .:......................	$ .10	$ .04
1¢ Franklin—Green	.20	.05
1½¢ Harding—Brown	.50	.06
2¢ Washington—Deep red	.20	.05
3¢ Lincoln—Purple............................	.35	.07

4¢	Martha Washington—Brown	2.00	.06
5¢	Theodore Roosevelt—Blue	1.25	.04
6¢	James Garfield—Deep orange	1.25	.04
7¢	William McKinley—Black	2.00	.07
8¢	Gen. Grant—Olive green	2.00	.05
9¢	Jefferson—Orange red or rose	2.25	.05
10¢	James Monroe—Orange	2.50	.07
11¢	Rutherford B. Hayes—Light blue	2.50	.07
12¢	Grover Cleveland—Brown violet	3.75	.06
13¢	Benjamin Harrison—Light green	1.50	.08
14¢	American Indian—Blue	2.75	.17
15¢	Statue of Liberty—Gray	7.50	.05
17¢	Woodrow Wilson—Black	3.50	.11
20¢	Golden Gate—Red	10.00	.05
25¢	Niagara Falls—Green	7.25	.08
30¢	Buffalo—Brown	16.50	.08
50¢	Arlington Amphitheater—Lilac	37.50	.08
$1	Lincoln Memorial—Violet black	37.50	.25

$2 U.S. Capitol—Blue	120.00	6.25
$5 Head of "America"—Red and blue	225.00	7.50
1¢ Franklin—Green, no perfs., wide margins	4.50	2.75
1½¢ Harding—Brown, no perfs., wide margins	1.25	1.00
2¢ Washington—Carmine, no perfs., wide margins ...	1.35	1.15

1922-38 SERIES, OVERPRINTED "KANS."

1¢ Franklin, side bust—Green	$1.50	$1.25
1½¢ Harding—Brown	2.50	1.50
2¢ Washington—Carmine	1.75	.30
3¢ Lincoln—Violet	12.50	8.75
4¢ Martha Washington—Brown	11.00	5.00
5¢ Theodore Roosevelt—Blue	9.00	6.50
6¢ James Garfield—Red orange	17.50	10.00
7¢ William McKinley—Black	18.50	15.00
8¢ General Grant—Olive green	55.00	40.00
9¢ Thomas Jefferson—Rose	9.00	6.00
10¢ James Monroe—Orange	15.00	6.00

1922-38 SERIES, OVERPRINTED "NEBR."

1¢ Franklin—Green	$1.50	$1.25
1½¢ Harding—Brown	1.75	1.35
2¢ Washington—Carmine	1.50	.60
3¢ Lincoln—Violet	9.00	5.75
4¢ Martha Washington—Brown	11.00	6.50
5¢ Theodore Roosevelt—Blue	10.00	6.50
6¢ James Garfield—Red orange	20.00	12.50
7¢ William McKinley—Black	12.50	10.00
8¢ General Grant—Olive Green	22.50	15.00
9¢ Thomas Jefferson—Rose	23.50	17.50
10¢ James Monroe—Orange	65.00	15.00

1923

1,459,487,085	2¢ Harding—Black, perforated 11 all around	$ .85	$ .10
99,950,300	Same—Perforated 10 all around	12.50	1.25
770,000	Same—No perforations, nice wide margins.......................	10.50	3.75

1924

Huguenot—Walloon Issue:

51,378,023	1¢ Ship "New Netherland"—Green....	$5.50	$4.50
77,753,423	2¢ Landing Fort Orange—Red	8.00	3.00
5,659,023	5¢ Monument at Mayport, Florida—Blue	45.00	17.50

Lexington-Concord Issue:

15,615,000	1¢ Gen. Washington at Cambridge—Green	$5.25	$4.25
26,596,600	2¢ The Birth of Liberty—Red	9.00	5.00
5,348,800	5¢ Minute Man—Blue	40.00	15.00

1925

Norse-American Issue:

9,104,983	2¢ Ship "Restoration"—Red, black	$8.50	$3.50
1,900,983	5¢ Viking Ship—Blue, black	20.00	12.50

1926

20,280,500	5¢ John Ericsson Memorial—Lilac	$11.00	$4.25
107,398	2¢ Liberty Bell, Sesquicentennial Exposition—Red	5.00	.60
40,639,485	2¢ Gun Battery, Battle of White Plains—Red	3.00	2.25
107,398	Same—Souvenir sheet of 25 stamps (See Illus. p. 47)	600.00	350.00

1927

39,974,900	2¢ Green Mountain Boy, Vermont Sesquicentennial—Red	$1.50	$1.25
25,628,450	2¢ Surrender of Gen. Burgoyne—Red . .	4.25	2.50

1928

101,330,328	2¢ Washington at Prayer, Valley Forge Sesquicentennial—Red	$1.00	$ .50

9,779,896	2¢ Washington Regular Issue with Overprint "Molly Pitcher," Battle of Monmouth—Red	1.50	1.25

Hawaii Discovery Sesquicentennial:

5,519,897	2¢ Washington Regular Issue with Overprint "Hawaii, 1778-1928"—Red .	$5.50	$4.25
1,459,897	5¢ Theodore Roosevelt, same overprint—Blue	18.50	15.00

International Civil Aeronautics Conference:

51,342,273	2¢ Wright Airplane—Red	$1.25	$1.00
10,319,700	5¢ Globe and Airplane—Blue	5.75	3.75

1929

16,684,674	2¢ Surrender of Fort Sackville, George Rogers Clark—Red and black	$ .75	$ .60
241,798,674	2¢ Edison's First Lamp, Electric Light Golden Jubilee—Red	1.00	.60
51,451,880.	2¢ Gen. John Sullivan—Red	.60	.50

29,338,274	2¢ Battle of Fallen Timbers—Carmine ..	1.00	.80
32,680,900	2¢ Ohio River Canalization—Carmine ..	.70	.50

1930

74,000,774	2¢ Massachusetts Bay Colony—Carmine	$ .60	$ .40
25,215,574	2¢ Carolina-Charleston—Carmine	1.00	.85
25,609,470	2¢ Battle of Braddock Field—Carmine ..	.90	.70
66,487,000	2¢ Gen. Von Steuben—Carmine	.60	.45

1931

96,559,400	2¢ Gen. Pulaski—Carmine	$ .30	$ .20
99,074,600	2¢ Red Cross—Black and red	.18	.15
25,006,400	2¢ Rochambeau, Washington and De Grasse, Yorktown—Black and red .	.30	.20

1932

Washington Bicentennial Issue

87,969,700	½¢ Miniature by Charles W. Peale—Brown	$ .08	$ .05
1,265,555,100	1¢ Bust by Jean A. Houdon—Green ...	.12	.04
304,926,800	1½¢ Painting by Peale—Light brown	.30	.05
4,222,198,300	2¢ Painting by Gilbert Stuart—Red	.12	.04
456,198,500	3¢ Painting by Peale—Violet	.30	.05
151,201,300	4¢ Painting by Peale—Brown	.30	.06
170,565,100	5¢ Painting by Peale—Blue	1.75	.07
111,739,400	6¢ Painting by John Trumbull—Orange .	3.00	.08
83,257,400	7¢ Painting by Trumbull—Black	.40	.10
96,506,100	8¢ Drawing by Charles Saint Memin— Olive bistre	3.75	.60

| 75,709,200 | 9¢ Drawing by W. Williams—Pale red . | 3.25 | .20 |
| 147,216,000 | 10¢ Portrait by Stuart—Orange yellow ... | 12.50 | .10 |

51,102,800	2¢ Ski Jumper, Olympic Winter Games—		
	Red	.35	.20
100,869,300	2¢ Arbor Day—Red	.20	.08

Xth Olympiad Issue:

| 168,885,300 | 3¢ Runner—Violet .... | $ .50 | $ .07 |
| 52,376,100 | 5¢ Discus Thrower—Blue .... | .85 | .20 |

—	3¢ Washington—Purple	.25	.03
49,949,000	3¢ William Penn—Violet............	.25	.12
49,538,500	3¢ Daniel Webster—Violet	.45	.25

1933

61,719,200	3¢ General Oglethorpe—Violet	$ .30	$ .15
73,382,400	3¢ Washington's Headquarters at New-		
	burgh—Purple	.15	.08

Century of Progress Issue:

348,266,800	1¢ Fort Dearborn—Green	$ .12	$ .05
2,467,800	Same—Without perfs., wide margins	.60	.45
456,704	Same—Without perfs., souvenir sheet		
	of 25 stamps	45.00	25.00
480,239,300	3¢ Federal Building—Violet	.15	.05
2,147,850	Same—Without perfs., wide margins	.60	.40
441,172	Same—Without perfs., souvenir sheet		
	of 25 stamps	37.50	20.00

1,978,707,300	3¢ National Recovery Act—Purple	.15	.04
811,404	3¢ Byrd Antarctic Expedition—Blue ...	.90	.70
	Same—No perfs., wide margins	3.00	2.00
	Same—Souvenir sheet of 6 stamps ..	20.00	15.00
45,137,700	5¢ Kosciuszko—Blue	.65	.25

1934

46,258,300	3¢ Maryland—Red	$ .22	$ .18
208,671,300	3¢ Mother's Day—Purple	.15	.05
2,389,288	Same—No perfs.................	.50	.50
64,525,400	3¢ Wisconsin Tercentenary—Purple	.25	.12
2,294,948	Same—No perfs.................	.50	.50

National Parks Issue:

84,896,350	1¢ Yosemite—Green	$ .10	$ .06
4,897,396	Same—No perfs.................	.15	.12
793,551	Same—Souvenir sheet of 6	12.50	8.50
74,400,200	2¢ Grand Canyon—Red	.12	.06
2,746,640	Same—No perfs.................	.18	.18

95,089,000	3¢ Mount Rainier—Purple	.15	.07
3,463,608	Same—No perfs.................	.50	.50
511,391	Same—Souvenir sheet of 6	30.00	20.00
19,178,650	4¢ Mesa Verde—Brown	.45	.35
1,822,686	Same—No perfs.................	.65	.55
30,980,100	5¢ Old Faithful—Blue	.90	.65
1,724,576	Same—No perfs.................	1.00	.85
16,923,350	6¢ Crater Lake—Blue	1.00	.75
1,647,696	Same—No perfs.................	1.25	1.00
15,988,250	7¢ Acadia Park—Black	.90	.65
1,682,948	Same—No perfs.................	1.00	.75
15,288,700	8¢ Zion Park—Olive green	1.75	1.50
1,638,644	Same—No perfs.................	1.10	.90
17,472,600	9¢ Glacier National Park—Orange	1.75	.60
1,625,224	Same—No perfs.................	1.10	.90
18,877,300	10¢ Great Smoky Mountains—Black	3.00	1.00
1,644,900	Same—No perfs.................	2.50	1.75

1935

70,726,800	3¢ Charter Oak (Connecticut Tercentenary)—Purple	$ .12	$ .06
100,389,600	3¢ California Exposition at San Diego—Purple	.12	.06
75,823,900	3¢ Michigan Centenary—Purple	.12	.06

| 73,610,650 | 3¢ Boulder Dam—Purple | $ .12 | $ .06 |

<h3 style="text-align:center">1936</h3>

| 124,324,500 | 3¢ Texas Centennial—Purple | $ .12 | $ .06 |
| 67,127,650 | 3¢ Roger Williams (Rhode Island Tercentenary)—Purple | .12 | .06 |

72,992,650	3¢ Arkansas Centennial—Purple	.12	.06
74,407,450	3¢ Oregon Territory—Purple	.12	.06
269,522,200	3¢ Susan B. Anthony—Purple	.12	.05
2,809,039	12¢ Souvenir Sheet of 4, with 3¢ Connecticut, 3¢ Texas, 3¢ San Diego and 3¢ Michigan—Purple	3.75	3.00

1936-37

Army Commemorative Issue

105,196,150	1¢ Washington and Greene—Green	$ .10	$ .06
93,848,500	2¢ Jackson and Scott—Red	.12	.06
87,741,150	3¢ Sherman, Grant and Sheridan—Purple	.18	.08
35,794,150	4¢ Lee and Jackson—Gray	.35	.12
36,839,250	5¢ West Point—Blue	.50	.12

Navy Commemorative Issue:

104,773,450	1¢ Jones and Barry—Green	.10	.06
92,054,550	2¢ Decatur and MacDonough—Red	.12	.06
93,291,650	3¢ Farragut and Porter—Purple	.18	.08
34,552,950	4¢ Sampson, Dewey and Schley—Gray .	.35	.12
36,819,050	5¢ Navy Cadets and Seal—Blue	.50	.12

1937

84,825,250	3¢ Map, Ordinance of 1787—Purple ...	$ .15	$ .06
25,040,400	5¢ Virginia Dare—Blue	.45	.25
5,277,445	10¢ Smoky Mountain National Park— Souvenir sheet—Green	1.25	.65
99,882,300	3¢ Signing of Constitution—Red violet .	.18	.07

78,454,450	3¢ Hawaii Territory—Purple	.15	.07
77,004,200	3¢ Alaska Territory—Purple	.15	.07
81,292,450	3¢ Puerto Rico Territory—Purple	.15	.07
76,474,550	3¢ Virgin Islands Territory—Violet	.15	.07

1938—REGULAR ISSUE PRESIDENTIAL SERIES

½¢ Franklin—Orange	$ .05	$ .05
1¢ Washington—Green	.06	.04
1½¢ Martha Washington—Brown	.06	.04
2¢ John Adams—Red	.07	.04
3¢ Thomas Jefferson—Purple	.10	.04
4¢ James Madison—Mauve	.25	.05
4½¢ White House—Gray	.20	.05
5¢ James Monroe—Blue	.25	.05
6¢ John Quincy Adams—Orange	.30	.05
7¢ Andrew Jackson—Chocolate	.35	.05

8¢	Martin Van Buren—Olive green	.35	.05
9¢	William H. Harrison—Pink	.40	.05
10¢	John Tyler—Orange	.35	.05
11¢	James Polk—Blue	.45	.08
12¢	Zachary Taylor—Violet	.80	.06
13¢	Millard Fillmore—Green	.80	.10
14¢	Franklin Pierce—Blue	.90	.10
15¢	James Buchanan—Gray	.65	.05
16¢	Abraham Lincoln—Black	1.00	.20
17¢	Andrew Johnson—Red brown	1.00	.10
18¢	Ulysses S. Grant—Brown	1.25	.10
19¢	Rutherford B. Hayes—Violet	1.25	.25
20¢	James Garfield—Green	1.00	.05
21¢	Chester A. Arthur—Blue	1.35	.12
22¢	Grover Cleveland—Orange red	1.35	.30
24¢	Benjamin Harrison—Gray black	2.25	.20
25¢	William McKinley—Red violet	1.35	.06
30¢	Theodore Roosevelt—Blue	7.00	.05
50¢	William H. Taft—Violet	10.00	.06

$1	Woodrow Wilson—Violet and black	17.50	.10
$2	Warren G. Harding—Green and black	45.00	4.50
$5	Calvin Coolidge—Red and black	175.00	1.75

1938

47,064,300	3¢ Constitution Ratification—Violet	$ .25	$ .08
58,564,368	3¢ Swedes and Finns Tercentenary—Red violet	.25	.10
65,939,500	3¢ Northwest Territory Sesquicentennial—Violet	.25	.08
47,064,300	3¢ Iowa Territory—Violet	.25	.08

1939

114,439,600	3¢ Golden Gate Exposition—Purple	$ .15	$ .06
101,699,550	3¢ New York World's Fair—Deep purple	.15	.06

72,764,550	3¢ Washington's Inauguration—Red violet	.25	.10
71,394,750	3¢ Printing Press—Violet	.15	.08

81,269,600	3¢ Baseball Centennial—Violet	.25	.08
67,813,350	3¢ Panama Canal—Red violet	.25	.08
66,835,000	3¢ States of North and South Dakota, Montana and Washington (50th Anniversaries)—Red violet	.15	.08

1940

Famous Americans Series:
Authors:

56,348,320	1¢ Washington Irving—Green	$ .08	$ .06
53,177,110	2¢ James F. Cooper—Red	.12	.08
53,260,270	3¢ Ralph W. Emerson—Red violet	.14	.06
22,104,950	5¢ Louisa May Alcott—Blue	.35	.20
13,201,270	10¢ Samuel L. Clemens—Brown	2.50	2.00

Poets:

51,603,580	1¢ Henry W. Longfellow—Green	$ .14	$ .08
52,100,510	2¢ John G. Whittier—Red	.12	.08
51,666,580	3¢ James R. Lowell—Red violet	.20	.06
22,207,780	5¢ Walt Whitman—Blue	.35	.25
11,835,530	10¢ James W. Riley—Brown	3.50	2.00

Educators:

52,471,160	1¢ Horace Mann—Green	$ .10	$ .08
52,366,440	2¢ Mark Hopkins—Red	.12	.07
51,636,270	3¢ Charles W. Eliot—Red violet	.35	.07
20,729,030	5¢ Frances E. Willard—Blue	.45	.25
14,125,580	10¢ Booker T. Washington—Brown	2.25	1.50

Scientists:

59,409,000	1¢ John J. Audubon—Green	$ .08	$ .07
57,888,600	2¢ Dr. C. W. Long—Red	.10	.07
28,273,180	3¢ Luther Burbank—Red violet	.12	.07
23,779,000	5¢ Dr. Walter Reed—Blue	.35	.25
15,112,580	10¢ Jane Addams—Brown	2.25	1.25

Composers:

57,322,790	1¢ Stephen Foster—Green	$ .08	$ .07
58,281,580	2¢ John P. Sousa—Red	.10	.07
56,398,790	3¢ Victor Herbert—Red violet	.15	.07
21,147,000	5¢ Edward A. MacDowell—Blue	.35	.25
13,328,000	10¢ Ethelbert Nevin—Brown	4.25	1.75

Artists:

54,389,510	1¢ Gilbert Stuart—Green	$ .08	$ .06
53,636,580	2¢ James A. M. Whistler—Red	.10	.06
55,313,230	3¢ Augustus Saint-Gaudens—Red violet	.12	.06
21,720,580	5¢ Daniel C. French—Blue	.35	.25
13,600,580	10¢ Frederick Remington—Brown	2.75	2.00

Inventors:

47,599,580	1¢ Eli Whitney—Green	$ .15	$ .08
53,766,510	2¢ Samuel F. B. Morse—Red	.12	.07
54,193,580	3¢ Cyrus H. McCormick—Red violet ..	.20	.06
207,264,580	5¢ Elias Howe—Blue	1.25	.40
13,726,580	10¢ Alexander G. Bell—Brown	10.00	3.00

47,700,000	3¢ Pan American Union—Light violet ..	.45	.15
50,034,400	3¢ Wyoming statehood—Brown violet ..	.20	.08
44,389,550	3¢ Emancipation—Deep violet	.30	.15

46,497,400	3¢ Pony Express—Red brown	.50	.15
50,618,150	3¢ Idaho Statehood—Violet	.20	.08
60,943,700	3¢ Coronado Expedition—Violet	.22	.08

Defense Issue:

6,081,409,300	1¢ Statue of Liberty—Green	$ .05	$ .04
5,211,708,200	2¢ Anti-aircraft Gun—Red	.07	.05
8,384,867,600	3¢ Liberty Torch—Violet	.12	.05

1941

54,574,550	3¢ Vermont Statehood—Violet	$ .22	$ .10

1942

63,558,400	3¢ Daniel Boone, Kentucky Statehood—Violet	$ .18	$ .10
20,642,793,300	3¢ Win the War—Violet	.12	.04
21,272,800	5¢ Lincoln, Sun Yat-Sen and Map of China—Blue	.50	.30

92

1943

1,671,564,200	2¢ Nations United for Victory—Red ...	$ .10	$ .05
1,227,334,200	1¢ Four Freedoms—Green............	.08	.05

1943-1944

Overrun Nations Series (see Illus. p. 43):

19,999,646	5¢ Flag of Poland—Multicolored	$ .30	$ .20
19,999,646	5¢ Flag of Czechoslovakia—Multicolored	.25	.15
19,999,646	5¢ Flag of Norway—Multicolored	.20	.15
19,999,646	5¢ Flag of Luxembourg—Multicolored .	.20	.15
19,999,646	5¢ Flag of Netherlands—Multicolored ..	.20	.15
19,999,646	5¢ Flag of Belgium—Multicolored	.20	.15
19,999,648	5¢ Flag of France—Multicolored	.20	.15
14,999,646	5¢ Flag of Greece—Multicolored	.40	.20
14,999,646	5¢ Flag of Yugoslavia—Multicolored ...	.35	.18
14,999,646	5¢ Flag of Albania—Multicolored	.35	.18
14,999,646	5¢ Flag of Austria—Multicolored	.35	.18
14,999,646	5¢ Flag of Denmark—Multicolored	.35	.18
14,999,646	5¢ Flag of Korea—Multicolored	.40	.22

1944

61,303,000	3¢ Transcontinental Railroad—Violet ...	$ .15	$ .10
61,001,450	3¢ First Steamship across the Atlantic—Violet	.15	.10
60,605,000	3¢ Telegraph Centenary—Red violet ...	.15	.10
50,129,350	3¢ Corregidor—Violet	.15	.10
53,479,400	3¢ Motion Picture Industry—Violet	.15	.10

1945

61,617,350	3¢ Florida Centennial—Red violet	$ .12	$ .08
75,500,000	5¢ United Nations—Blue	.15	.08
137,321,000	3¢ Iwo Jima—Green	.12	.05

Roosevelt Memorial Issue

128,140,000	1¢ F.D.R. and Hyde Park—Green	$ .06	$ .05
67,255,000	2¢ F.D.R. and Warm Springs—Red	.10	.07
138,870,000	3¢ F.D.R. and White House—Violet ...	.12	.07
76,455,400	5¢ F.D.R. and Four Freedoms—Blue ...	.15	.08

128,357,750	3¢ U.S. Army—Olive	.12	.05
138,863,000	3¢ U.S. Navy—Blue	.12	.05
111,616,700	3¢ Coast Guard—Green	.12	.05
308,587,700	3¢ Al Smith—Purple	.12	.04
170,640,000	3¢ Texas—Blue	.12	.05

1946

135,927,000	3¢ Merchant Marine—Green	$ .12	$ .05
269,339,100	3¢ Discharge Emblem—Violet	.12	.04
132,274,500	3¢ Tennessee Statehood—Violet	.12	.05
132,430,000	3¢ Iowa Statehood—Blue	.12	.05
139,209,500	3¢ Smithsonian Institute—Brown	.12	.05
114,684,450	3¢ Kearny Expedition—Brown violet ...	.12	.05

1947

156,540,510	3¢ Edison—Red violet	$ .12	$ .05
120,452,600	3¢ Joseph Pulitzer—Purple	.12	.05
127,104,300	3¢ Postage Stamp Centenary—Blue	.12	.05
127,104,300	3¢ The Doctor—Brown violet	.12	.05
131,968,000	3¢ Utah Centennial—Violet	.12	.05
131,488,000	3¢ Frigate "Constitution"—Green	.12	.05
122,362,000	3¢ Florida Everglades—Green	.12	.05
10,299,600	15¢ Souvenir sheet with Reproductions of First U.S. Stamps, 5¢ Franklin and 10¢ Washington—Blue and orange	2.25	1.00

1948

121,548,000	3¢ George W. Carver—Red violet	$ .12	$ .05
131,109,500	3¢ California Gold Centennial—Violet . .	.12	.05
122,650,500	3¢ Mississippi Territory—Brown violet .	.12	.05
77,649,600	3¢ William Allen White—Red violet . . .	.12	.06
121,953,500	3¢ Four chaplains—Black	.12	.05

115,250,000	3¢ Wisconsin Centennial—Violet	.12	.05
64,198,500	5¢ Swedish Pioneers—Blue	.18	.10
117,642,500	3¢ Progress of Women—Violet	.12	.05
113,474,500	3¢ U.S.-Canada Friendship—Blue	.12	.05
120,868,500	3¢ Francis Scott Key—Red	.12	.05
77,800,500	3¢ Salute to Youth—Blue	.12	.05
52,214,000	3¢ Oregon Territory—Brown red	.15	.10
53,958;100	3¢ Harlan Stone—Red violet	.15	.10
61,120,010	3¢ Palomar Observatory—Blue	.25	.10
57,823,000	3¢ Clara Barton, American Red Cross—Red	.12	.07

52,975,000	3¢ Poultry Industry—Brown	.15	.08
58,332,000	3¢ Fort Kearny—Violet	.12	.08
56,228,000	3¢ Volunteer Firemen—Red	.12	.08
57,832,000	3¢ Indian Tribes—Brown	.12	.08
53,875,000	3¢ Rough Riders—Violet brown	.15	.10

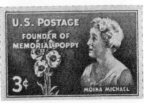

63,834,000	3¢ Girl Scouts—Green	.12	.08
67,162,200	3¢ Will Rogers—Red violet	.12	.08
64,561,000	3¢ Fort Bliss—Red brown	.30	.08
64,079,500	3¢ Moina Michael—Red	.12	.08
63,388,000	3¢ Gettysburg Address—Blue	.12	.08

62,285,000	3¢ American Turners—Red	.12	.08
57,492,610	3¢ Joel Chandler Harris—Red violet . . .	.12	.08
77,149,000	3¢ Gold Star Mothers—Yellow	.12	.08

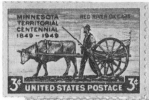  

1949

99,190,000	3¢ Minnesota Territory—Green	$ .12	$ .05
104,790,000	3¢ Washington and Lee University—Blue	.12	.05
108,805,000	3¢ Puerto Rico Elections—Green	.12	.05
107,340,000	3¢ Annapolis—Light blue	.12	.05
117,020,000	3¢ G.A.R.—Red	.12	.05
122,633,000	3¢ Edgar A. Poe—Red violet	.12	.05

1950

130,960,000	3¢ American Bankers Association—Green	$ .12	$ .05
128,478,000	3¢ Samuel Gompers—Red violet	.12	.05
122,315,000	3¢ Railroad Engineers—Brown	.12	.05

National Capital Sesquicentennial Issue:

132,090,000	3¢ Statue of Freedom—Blue	$ .12	$ .05
130,050,000	3¢ White House—Green	.12	.05
131,350,000	3¢ Supreme Court—Violet	.12	.05
129,980,000	3¢ U.S. Capitol—Red violet	.12	.05

122,170,000	3¢ Kansas City Centennial—Violet	.12	.05
131,635,000	3¢ Boy Scouts—Dark brown	.12	.05
121,860,000	3¢ Indiana Territory—Blue	.12	.05
121,120,000	3¢ California Statehood—Yellow orange	.12	.05

1951

119,120,000	3¢ Confederate Veterans—Gray	$ .12	$ .05
112,125,000	3¢ Nevada Centennial—Green	.12	.05
114,140,000	3¢ Detroit—Blue	.12	.05

114,490,000	3¢ Colorado Statehood—Blue violet	.12	.05
117,200,000	3¢ Chemical Society—**Violet brown**	.12	.05
116,130,000	3¢ Battle of Brooklyn—Violet	.12	.05

1952

116,175,000	3¢ Betsy Ross—Red	$ .12	$ .05
115,945,000	3¢ 4-H Clubs—Green	.12	.05
112,540,000	3¢ B. & O. Railway—Blue	.12	.05
117,415,000	3¢ American Automobile Association—		
	Blue	.12	.05
2,899,580,000	3¢ N.A.T.O.—Violet	.12	.05
114,540,000	3¢ Grand Coulee Dam—Green	.12	.05
113,135,000	3¢ Lafayette—Blue	.12	.05
116,255,000	3¢ Mount Rushmore—Green	.12	.05
113,860,000	3¢ Civil Engineers—Blue	.12	.05

124,260,000	3¢ Service Women—Blue	.12	.05
115,735,000	3¢ Gutenberg Bible—Violet	.12	.05
115,430,000	3¢ Newsboys—Violet	.12	.05
136,220,000	3¢ Red Cross—Red and blue	.12	.05

1953

114,894,600	3¢ National Guard—Blue	$ .10	$ .05
118,706,000	3¢ Ohio Statehood—Brown	.10	.05
114,190,000	3¢ Washington Territory—Green	.10	.05
113,990,000	3¢ Louisiana Purchase—Violet brown	.12	.05
82,289,600	5¢ Perry and Japan—Green	.18	.10
114,865,000	3¢ American Bar Association—Violet	.12	.05
115,780,000	3¢ Sagamore Hill—Green	.12	.05
115,244,600	3¢ Future Farmers of America—Blue	.12	.05
123,709,600	3¢ Trucking Industry—Violet	.12	.05

144,789,600	3¢ General Patton—Violet	.12	.05
115,759,600	3¢ New York City Tercentenary—Red violet	.12	.05
116,134,600	3¢ Gadsden Purchase—Brown	.12	.05

1954—COMMEMORATIVES

118,540,000	3¢ Columbia University—Blue	$ .12	$ .05
115,840,000	3¢ Nebraska Territory—Violet	.12	.05
113,603,700	3¢ Kansas Territory—Orange	.12	.05
121,100,000	3¢ George Eastman—Brown	.12	.05
116,078,150	3¢ Lewis & Clark Expedition—Brown	.12	.05

1954-65—REGULAR ISSUE PATRIOTIC SERIES

½¢ Franklin—Orange	$ .05	$ .03
1¢ Washington—Green	.05	.03
1¼¢ Palace of Governors—Turquoise	.07	.05
1½¢ Mount Vernon—Brown	.08	.04
2¢ Jefferson—Red	.06	.03

2½¢	Bunker Hill—Gray blue	.09	.05
3¢	Statue of Liberty—Violet	.08	.03
4¢	Lincoln—Red violet	.12	.03
4½¢	Hermitage—Blue green	.15	.08
5¢	James Monroe—Blue	.15	.04
6¢	Theodore Roosevelt—Red	.18	.04
7¢	Woodrow Wilson—Carmine red	.25	.05
8¢	Statue of Liberty—Red and blue	.30	.05
	Same—Torch below "U.S. Postage"	.25	.05
8¢	Gen. Pershing—Brown	.25	.05
9¢	Alamo—Pink	.25	.05

103

10¢ Independence Hall—Brown	.30	.04
11¢ Statue of Liberty—Red and blue	.30	.05
12¢ Harrison—Red	.40	.05
15¢ John Jay—Rose lake..........................	.45	.05
20¢ Monticello—Blue	.65	.05
25¢ Paul Revere—Green	1.00	.06
30¢ Lee—Black	1.50	.08
40¢ John Marshall—Brown red	2.50	.10
50¢ Susan B. Anthony—Violet.....................	2.75	.06
$1 Patrick Henry—Purple	8.50	.10
$5 Alexander Hamilton—Black	125.00	2.75

1955

116,139,800	3¢ Pennsylvania Academy of Fine Arts— Rose brown	$ .12	$ .05
120,484,800	3¢ Land Grant Colleges—Green	.12	.05
53,854,750	8¢ Rotary International—Deep blue	.25	.11
176,075,000	3¢ Armed Forces Reserve—Purple	.12	.05
125,944,400	3¢ Old Man of the Mountains—Green ..	.12	.05
122,284,600	3¢ Soo Locks—Blue	.12	.05

133,638,850	3¢ Atoms for Peace—Deep blue	.25	.05
118,664,600	3¢ Fort Ticonderoga—Light brown	.12	.05
112,434,000	3¢ Andrew Mellon—Rose carmine	.12	.05

1956

129,384,550	3¢ Benjamin Franklin—Bright carmine .	$ .12	$ .05
121,184,600	3¢ Booker T. Washington's Birthplace—Deep blue	.12	.05
119,784,200	3¢ FIPEX (Fifth International Philatelic Exhibition)—Deep violet	.12	.05
9,802,025	11¢ FIPEX Souvenir Sheet, 3¢ and 8¢ Statue of Liberty—Deep violet	6.25	3.75

Wildlife Conservation Issue:

123,159,400	3¢ Wild Turkey—Rose lake	$ .12	$ .05
123,138,800	3¢ Pronghorn Antelope—Brown	.12	.05
109,275,000	3¢ King Salmon—Blue green	.12	.05

| 119,932,200 | 3¢ Pure Food and Drug Laws—Dark blue-green. . . . . | .12 | .05 |

| 125,475,000 | 3¢ Wheatland—Black brown . . . . | .12 | .05 |
| 117,855,000 | 3¢ Labor Day—Deep blue . . . . | .12 | .05 |

122,100,000	3¢ Nassau Hall, Princeton—Orange	.12	.05
118,180,000	3¢ Devil's Tower—Violet	.12	.05
100,975,000	3¢ Children's Stamp—Dark blue	.12	.05

1957

115,299,450	3¢ Hamilton—Rose red	$ .12	$ .05
186,949,250	3¢ Polio Fighters—Red lilac	.12	.05
115,235,000	3¢ Coast and Geodetic Survey—Deep blue	.12	.05
120,010,000	3¢ Steel Industry—Bright ultramarine . .	.12	.05
106,647,500	3¢ American Institute of Architects—Red lilac	.12	.05
118,399,600	3¢ International Naval Review—Blue-green	.12	.05

102,219,500	3¢ Oklahoma Statehood—Dark blue	.12	.05
103,045,000	3¢ Teachers of America—Rose lake	.12	.05
84,054,400	4¢ American Flag (48 stars)—Dark blue and deep carmine	.15	.08

126,266,000	3¢ Shipbuilding—Deep violet	.12	.05
39,489,600	8¢ Ramon Magsaysay (Champions of Liberty Series)—Carmine, ultra-marine and ochre	.25	.15
122,990,000	3¢ Lafayette—Rose lake	.12	.05

174,372,800	3¢ Whooping Crane, Wildlife Conservation—Blue, ochre and green	.12	.05
114,365,000	3¢ Flushing Remonstrance—Black	.12	.05

1958

122,765,200	3¢ Gardening and Horticulture—Green .	$ .12	$ .05

125,815,200	3¢ Brussels Exhibition—Deep claret	.12	.05
120,196,580	3¢ Monroe—Purple	.12	.05
120,805,200	3¢ Minnesota Statehood—Green	.12	.05
125,815,200	3¢ International Geophysical Year—Black and red orange	.25	.05
108,415,200	3¢ Gunston Hall—Light green	.12	.05
107,195,200	3¢ Mackinac Straits Bridge—Bright greenish blue	.12	.05

115,745,280	4¢ Simon Bolivar (Champions of Liberty Series)—Olive bistre	.12	.05
39,743,640	8¢ Same—Carmine, ultramarine and ochre	.30	.15

120,561,280	4¢ Lajos Kossuth (Champions of Liberty Series)—Green	.12	.05
44,664,576	8¢ Same—Carmine, ultramarine and ochre	.25	.12
114,570,200	4¢ Atlantic Cable—Red violet	.12	.05
114,860,200	4¢ Lincoln-Douglas Debates—Sepia	.12	.05
118,390,200	4¢ Freedom of the Press—Black	.12	.05
125,770,200	4¢ Overland Mail—Crimson rose	.12	.05

114,114,280	4¢ Noah Webster—Dark carmine rose . .	.12	.05
156,600,200	4¢ Forest Conservation—Green, yellow and brown	.12	.05
124,200,200	4¢ Fort Duquesne—Blue	.12	.05

1959

Lincoln Birth Year Centennial:

120,400,200	1¢ Painting by George P. A. Healey— Green	$ .07	$ .05
91,160,200	3¢ Bust by Gutzon Borglum—Purple . . .	.12	.05
126,500,000	4¢ Statue by Daniel Chester French— Blue	.12	.05

120,740,200	4¢	Oregon Statehood—Blue green	.12	.05
133,623,280	4¢	Jose de San Martin (Champions of Liberty Series)—Blue	.12	.05
45,569,088	8¢	Same—Carmine, ultramarine and ochre	.25	.12
122,493,280	4¢	NATO 10th Anniversary—Blue	.12	.05
131,260,000	4¢	Arctic Explorations—Bright greenish blue	.12	.05

1959 COMMEMORATIVES

47,125,200	8¢	"World Peace Through World Trade"—Rose lake	$ .25	$ .12

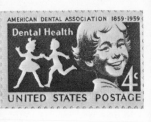

123,105,000	4¢	Silver Discovery Centennial—Black	.12	.05

126,105,050	4¢ St. Lawrence Seaway—Red and dark blue	.12	.05
209,170,000	4¢ American Flag (49 stars)—Ochre, dark blue and carmine	.12	.05
120,835,000	4¢ Soil Conservation—Blue, green and ochre	.12	.05
115,715,000	4¢ Petroleum Industry—Brown	.12	.05
118,445,000	4¢ Dental Health—Green	.12	.05

111,685,000	4¢ Ernst Reuter (Champions of Liberty Series)—Gray	.12	.05
43,099,200	8¢ Same—Carmine, ultramarine and ochre	.25	.12
115,444,000	4¢ Dr. Ephraim McDowell—Rose lake .	.12	.05

1960

American Credo Series:

126,470,000	4¢ Washington—Dark violet-blue and carmine	$ .20	$ .05
124,560,000	4¢ Franklin—Olive bistre and green	.20	.05
115,455,000	4¢ Jefferson—Gray and vermilion	.20	.05
122,060,000	4¢ Francis Scott Key—Carmine and dark blue	.20	.05
120,540,000	4¢ Lincoln—Magenta and green	.20	.05
113,075,000	4¢ Patrick Henry (1961)—Green and brown	.20	.05

139,125,000	4¢ Boy Scouts—Red, dark blue and bistre	.12	.05
124,445,000	4¢ Olympic Winter Games—Dull blue ..	.12	.05
113,792,000	4¢ Thomas Masaryk (Champions of Liberty Series)—Blue	.12	.05
44,215,200	8¢ Same—Carmine, ultramarine and ochre	.25	.12
113,195,000	4¢ World Refugee Year—Gray black ...	.12	.05
115,353,000	4¢ SEATO—Blue	.12	.05
121,805,000	4¢ Water Conservation—Dark blue, orange and green	.12	.05

111,080,000	4¢ American Woman—Deep violet		.12	.05
119,665,000	4¢ Pony Express—Sepia		.12	.05
153,025,000	4¢ American Flag (50 stars)—Dark blue and red		.12	.05
117,855,000	4¢ "Employ the Handicapped"—Dark blue.........................		.12	.05
118,185,000	4¢ World Forestry Congress—Green ...		.12	.05
112,260,000	4¢ Mexican Independence—Green and rose red		.12	.05

125,010,000	4¢ U.S.-Japan Treaty—Blue and pink ..		.12	.05
119,798,000	4¢ Ignace Jan Paderewski (Champions of Liberty Series)—Blue		.12	.05
42,696,000	8¢ Same—Carmine, ultramarine and ochre		.25	.12
115,171,000	4¢ Robert A. Taft—Dull violet		.12	.05
109,695,000	4¢ Wheels of Freedom—Dark blue		.12	.05
123,690,000	4¢ Boys' Clubs of America—Indigo, slate and rose red		.12	.05
127,970,000	4¢ First Automated Post Office—Dark blue and carmine		.12	.05

124,796,000	4¢ Baron Gustaf Mannerheim (Champions of Liberty Series)—Blue	.12	.05
42,076,800	8¢ Same—Carmine, ultramarine and ochre	.25	.12
116,215,000	4¢ Camp Fire Girls—Dark blue and bright red	.12	.05
126,252,000	4¢ Giuseppe Garibaldi (Champions of Liberty Series)—Green	.12	.05
42,746,000	8¢ Same—Carmine, ultramarine and ochre	.25	.12
125,290,000	4¢ Echo I—Deep violet	.65	.12
124,117,000	4¢ Senator Walter F. George—Dull violet	.12	.05
119,840,000	4¢ Andrew Carnegie—Deep claret	.12	.05
117,187,000	4¢ John Foster Dulles—Dull violet	.12	.05

1961

112,966,000	4¢ Mahatma Gandhi (Champions of Liberty Series)—Red orange	$ .12	$ .05
	8¢ Same—Carmine, ultramarine and ochre	.25	.12

110,850,000	4¢ Range Conservation—Blue, slate and brown orange	.12	.05
98,616,000	4¢ Horace Greeley—Dull violet	.12	.05
101,125,000	4¢ Fort Sumter—Light green	.20	.06
106,210,000	4¢ Kansas Statehood—Brown, dark red and green	.12	.05
110,810,000	4¢ Senator George W. Norris—Blue green	.12	.05

116,995,000	4¢ Naval Aviation—Blue	.12	.05
121,015,000	4¢ Workmen's Compensation Law—Ultramarine	.12	.05
111,600,000	4¢ Frederic Remington—Multicolored ..	.18	.05
110,620,000	4¢ Republic of China—Blue	.12	.05
109,110,000	4¢ Naismith-Basketball—Brown	.12	.05
145,350,000	4¢ Nursing Profession—Blue, green, orange and black	.12	.05

1962

112,870,000	4¢ New Mexico Statehood—Light blue, maroon and bistre	$ .12	$ .05
121,820,000	4¢ Arizona Statehood—Carmine, violet, blue and green	.18	.05
289,240,000	4¢ Project Mercury—Dark blue and yellow	.35	.10
120,155,000	4¢ Malaria Eradication—Blue and bistre	.12	.05
124,865,000	4¢ Battle of Shiloh—Black on peach ...	.15	.05
124,595,000	4¢ Charles Evans Hughes—Buff	.12	.05
147,310,000	4¢ Seattle World's Fair—Red and dark blue	.12	.05

| 118,690,000 | 4¢ Louisiana Statehood—Blue, dark slate green and red .... | .12 | .05 |
| 122,730,000 | 4¢ Homestead Act—Slate .... | .12 | .05 |

126,515,000	4¢ Girl Scouts—Red	.12	.05
130,960,000	4¢ Senator Brien McMahon—Purple ...	.12	.05
120,055,000	4¢ National Apprenticeship—Buff	.12	.05
120,715,000	4¢ Sam Rayburn—Brown and buff	.12	.05
121,440,000	4¢ Dag Hammarskjold—Yellow, brown and black	.12	.05
861,979,000	4¢ Wreath and Candles (Christmas Stamp)—Green and red	.12	.05
120,035,000	4¢ Higher Education—Blue, green and black	.12	.05
40,270,000	4¢ Hammarskjold (yellow background inverted)—Black, brown and yellow) (see Illus. p. 55)	.20	.10
117,870,000	4¢ Winslow Homer—Multicolored	.20	.05

1962-63 Regular Issue

1¢	Andrew Jackson—Green	$ .06	$ .03
5¢	Washington—Blue	.12	.04
5¢	American Flag Stamp—Red and blue	.12	.04

1963

129,945,000	5¢ Carolina Charter—Dark carmine and brown	$ .15	$ .05
135,620,000	5¢ Food for Peace—Green, buff and red	.15	.07
137,540,000	5¢ West Virginia Statehood—Green, red and black	.15	.05
79,905,000	5¢ Battle of Gettysburg—Blue and gray	.15	.05
132,435,000	5¢ Emancipation Proclamation—Dark blue, black and red	.15	.05
135,520,000	5¢ Alliance for Progress—Ultramarine and green.........................	.15	.05
131,420,000	5¢ Cordell Hull—Blue green	.15	.05
133,170,000	5¢ Eleanor Roosevelt—Bright purple ...	.15	.05

130,195,000	5¢ National Academy of Science—Prussian blue and black	.20	.05
118,665,000	5¢ Red Cross—Bluish black and red	.15	.05
128,450,000	5¢ City Mail Delivery—Gray, dark blue and red	.15	.05
1,291,250,000	5¢ Christmas Tree and White House, Christmas Stamp—Dark blue, bluish black and red	.15	.05
175,175,000	5¢ John James Audubon—Blue, brown and bistre	.20	.05

1964

125,995,000	5¢ Sam Houston—Black	$ .15	$ .05
128,025,000	5¢ Charles M. Russell—Multicolored	.20	.05
145,700,000	5¢ New York World's Fair—Blue-green	.20	.05

120,310,000	5¢ John Muir—Brown, green and olive .	.15	.05
125,410,000	5¢ Battle of the Wilderness—Dark red and black	.15	.05
511,750,000	5¢ Kennedy Memorial—Blue gray	.15	.05
123,845,000	5¢ New Jersey Tercentenary—Bright ultramarine	.15	.05
122,825,000	5¢ Nevada Statehood—Red, yellow and blue	.15	.05
325,000,000	5¢ Register and vote—Dark blue and red	.15	.05
123,245,000	5¢ Shakespeare—Brown, tan	.15	.05

123,355,000	5¢ Doctors Mayo—Green	.15	.05
126,970,000	5¢ American Music—Red, black and blue	.15	.05
121,250,000	5¢ Homemakers—Multicolored	.15	.05
120,005,000	5¢ Verrazano-Narrows Bridge—Green ..	.15	.05

Christmas Issue

351,552,000	5¢ Holly—Red and green	$1.00	$ .05
351,552,000	5¢ Mistletoe—Red and green	1.00	.05
351,552,000	5¢ Poinsettia—Red and green	1.00	.05
351,552,000	5¢ Pine Cone—Red and green	1.00	.05
125,800,000	5¢ Painting by Stuart Davis—Ultramarine, red and black	.15	.05
122,230,000	5¢ Amateur Radio—Red lilac	.15	.05

1965

115,095,000	5¢ Discus Thrower, Physical Fitness— Maroon and black	.15	.05
119,560,000	5¢ Crusade against Cancer—Black, purple and red orange	.15	.05
112,845,000	5¢ Appomattox—Prussian blue and black	.20	.05
125,180,000	5¢ Churchill Memorial—Black	.15	.05

115,695,000	5¢ Battle of New Orleans—Deep carmine, violet blue and gray	.15	.05
120,135,000	5¢ Magna Carta—Black, yellow ochre and red lilac	.15	.05
115,405,000	5¢ International cooperation—Dull blue and black	.15	.05

| 115,855,000 | 5¢ Salvation Army—Red, black and dark blue | .15 | .05 |

115,340,000	5¢ Dante—Maroon and tan	.15	.05
114,840,000	5¢ Herbert Hoover—Red	.15	.05
116,900,000	5¢ Settlement of Florida—Red, yellow and black	.15	.05
116,140,000	5¢ Robert Fulton—Black and blue	.15	.05
114,085,000	5¢ Traffic Safety—Green, red and black	.15	.05
114,880,000	5¢ Painting by John Copley—Black, brown and olive	.15	.05

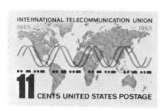  

26,995,000	11¢ International Telecommunication Union—Yellow, red and black	.50	.15
128,495,000	5¢ Adlai E. Stevenson—Multicolored . .	.15	.05
1,139,430,000	5¢ Angel with Trumpet (Christmas Stamp)—Red and green	.15	.05

1965-68—REGULAR ISSUE PROMINENT AMERICANS SERIES

1¢ Thomas Jefferson—Green	$ .04	$ .03
1¼¢ Albert Gallatin—Green	.15	.04
2¢ Frank Lloyd Wright—Slate blue	.05	.03
3¢ Francis Parkman—Purple	.07	.03

4¢ Lincoln—Black	.09	.04
5¢ Washington—Deep blue	.12	.05
5¢ Washington—Deep blue (redesigned)	.10	.02
6¢ Franklin D. Roosevelt—Gray brown	.12	.04

8¢ Albert Einstein—Violet	.25	.05
10¢ Andrew Jackson—Lilac	.20	.03
12¢ Henry Ford and Model T Ford—Black	.25	.04
13¢ John F. Kennedy—Brown	.25	.05
15¢ Oliver Wendell Holmes—Rose claret	.30	.04
20¢ George C. Marshall—Olive green	.35	.04
25¢ Frederick Douglass—Rose lake	.50	.04
30¢ John Dewey—Light purple	.55	.06
40¢ Thomas Paine—Dark blue	.75	.08
50¢ Lucy Stone—Maroon	.85	.05
$1 Eugene O'Neill—Purple	2.00	.10
$5 John Bassett Moore—Gray	10.00	2.25

| 116,835,000 | 5¢ Migratory Bird Treaty—Red and blue | $ .15 | $ .05 |
| 117,470,000 | 5¢ Humane Treatment of Animals—Orange-brown and black .... | .15 | .05 |

123,770,000	5¢ Indiana Statehood—Blue, yellow and brown	.15	.05
131,270,000	5¢ American Circus—Red, blue, pink and black	.15	.05
122,285,000	5¢ SIPEX (Sixth International Philatelic Exhibition)—Multicolored	.15	.05
14,680,000	5¢ SIPEX Souvenir sheet—Multicolored	.35	.20
114,160,000	5¢ Bill of Rights—Red, dark blue and light blue	.15	.05
128,475,000	5¢ Polish Millennium—Red	.15	.05

119,535,000	5¢ National Park Service—Yellow, black and green	.15	.05
125,110,000	5¢ Marine Corps Reserve—Black, red, blue and olive	.15	.05
114,853,200	5¢ General Federation of Women's Clubs—Blue, pink and black	.15	.05

PLANT for a more BEAUTIFUL AMERICA

WE APPRECIATE OUR SERVICEMEN

UNITED STATES SAVINGS BONDS
25TH ANNIVERSARY 5c

124,290,000	5¢ Johnny Appleseed—Red, black and green	.15	.05
128,460,000	5¢ Beautification of America—Emerald, pink and black	.18	.05
127,585,000	5¢ Great River Road—Yellow, red, black and green	.18	.05
115,875,000	5¢ Serviceman and Savings Bonds—Red, light blue and dark blue	.15	.05
1,173,547,420	5¢ Madonna and Child (Christmas Stamp)—Multicolored	.15	.05
114,015,000	5¢ Painting by Mary Cassatt—Multicolored	.20	.05

1967

121,105,000	5¢ National Grange—Orange, yellow, black, brown and green	$ .15	$ .05
132,045,000	5¢ Canada Centennial—Green, light blue, dark blue and black	.15	.05
118,780,000	5¢ Erie Canal Sesquicentennial—Light blue, dark blue, red and black	.15	.05

121,985,000	5¢ Search for Peace—Lions International—Red, blue and black	.15	.05
111,850,000	5¢ Henry David Thoreau—Black, red and green	.15	.05
117,225,000	5¢ Nebraska Statehood—Yellow, green and brown	.15	.05
111,515,000	5¢ Voice of America—Red, blue and black	.15	,05
114,270,000	5¢ Davy Crockett—Green and black ...	.15	.05

Space Accomplishment Twin Stamps:

60,432,500	5¢ Space-walking Astronaut—Light blue, dark blue, red and black	$2.50	$ .25
60,432,500	5¢ Gemini 4 Capsule and Earth—Light blue, dark blue, red and black (see Illus. p. 57)	2.50	.25
	Attached pairs	6.00	2.25
110,675,000	5¢ Urban Planning—Black and blue	.15	.05

110,670,000	5¢ Finland's Independence—Blue	.20	.05
113,825,000	5¢ Painting by Thomas Eakins—Multicolored	.20	.05
1,208,700,000	5¢ Madonna and Child (Christmas Stamp)—Multicolored	.15	.05
113,330,000	5¢ Mississippi Statehood—Multicolored	.20	.05

1968

	6¢ Flag and White House—Red, blue and green	$ .15	$ .04
141,350,000	6¢ Illinois Statehood—Blue, red and ochre	.20	.05

144,345,000	6¢ Hemisfair '68—Blue and pink	.20	.05
130,125,000	6¢ Law and Order—Gray-blue, red and black	.20	.05
147,120,000	6¢ Support Our Youth—Ultramarine and light red	.20	.05
158,700,000	6¢ Register and Vote—Gold and black .	.20	.05

Historical Flags Issue:

22,804,000	6¢ Fort Moultrie Flag, 1776—Ultramarine	$ .75	$ .30

22,804,000	6¢ Fort McHenry Flag, 1795-1818—Red and ultramarine	.75	.30
22,804,000	6¢ Washington's Cruisers Flag, 1775—Green and ultramarine	.75	.30
22,804,000	6¢ Bennington Flag, 1777—Red and ultramarine	.75	.30
22,804,000	6¢ Rhode Island Flag, 1775—Ultramarine yellow and red	.75	.30
22,804,000	6¢ First Stars and Stripes, 1777—Red and ultramarine	.75	.30
22,804,000	6¢ Bunker Hill Flag, 1775—Ultramarine, red and green	.75	.30
22,804,000	6¢ Grand Union Flag, 1776—Red and ultramarine	.75	.30
22,804,000	6¢ Philadelphia Light Horse Flag, 1775—Ultramarine, red and yellow	.75	.30
22,804,000	6¢ First Navy Jack, 1775—Red, yellow and ultramarine	.75	.30

153,015,000	6¢ Walt Disney—Multicolored	.20	.05
132,560,000	6¢ Father Marquette—Multicolored	.20	.05
130,385,000	6¢ Daniel Boone—Yellow, black and red	.20	.05

132,265,000	6¢ Arkansas River Navigation—Black and blue	.20	.05
128,710,000	6¢ Leif Erikson—Blackish brown and light grayish brown	.20	.05
124,775,000	6¢ Cherokee Strip Land Rush—Brown . .	.20	.05
128,295,000	6¢ Painting by John Trumbull—Multicolored	.20	.05

142,245,000	6¢ Wood Ducks, Wildlife Conservation—Multicolored	.30	.05
1,410,580,000	6¢ "The Annunciation" (Christmas Stamp)—Multicolored	.20	.05
125,100,000	6¢ American Indian—Multicolored	.30	.05

1969

Beautification of America Issue: sets of four

48,142,500	6¢ Beautiful Cities—Multicolored	$2.00	$ .10
48,142,500	6¢ Beautiful Parks—Multicolored	2.00	.10
48,142,500	6¢ Beautiful Highways—Multicolored . .	2.00	.10
48,142,500	6¢ Beautiful Streets—Multicolored	2.00	.10

148,770,000	6¢ American Legion—Multicolored	.20	.05
139,475,000	6¢ Painting by Grandma Moses—Multicolored	.25	.05
187,165,000	6¢ Apollo 8 Moon Orbit—Multicolored .	.50	.05
125,555,000	6¢ W.C. Handy—Multicolored	.20	.05
144,425,000	6¢ Settlement of California—Multicolored	.20	.05
135,875,000	6¢ John Wesley Powell—Multicolored ..	.20	.05
151,110,000	6¢ Alabama Statehood—Multicolored ..	.20	.05

XI International Botanical Congress Issue:

39,798,250	6¢ Douglas Fir—Multicolored	$ 2.50	$ .15
39,728,750	6¢ Ladyslipper—Multicolored	2.50	.15

39,728,750	6¢ Ocotillo—Multicolored	1.25	.10
38,728,750	6¢ Franklinia—Multicolored	1.25	.10

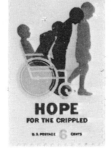

129,540,000	6¢ Daniel Webster, Dartmouth College Case—Green	.20	.05
130,925,000	6¢ Professional Baseball Centenary—Yellow-green and red	.25	.05
130,055,000	6¢ Intercollegiate Football Centenary—Green and red	.25	.05
150,611,200	6¢ Eisenhower Memorial—Blue, red and black (see Illus. p. 58)	.25	.05
1,709,795,000	6¢ "Winter Sunday in Norway, Maine" (Christmas Stamp)—Multicolored	.20	.05
127,545,000	6¢ Rehabilitation of Crippled Children and Adults—Multicolored	.20	.05
145,788,800	6¢ Painting by William M. Harnett—Multicolored	.25	.05

1970

Natural History Issue (see Illus. p. 59).

50,448,500	6¢ American Bald Eagle—Multicolored	$ .40	$ .08
50,448,500	6¢ African Elephant Herd—Multicolored	.40	.08
50,448,500	6¢ Haida Ceremonial Canoe—Multicolored	.40	.08
50,448,500	6¢ The Age of Reptiles—Multicolored	.40	.08

137,660,000	6¢ Edgar Lee Masters—Black and brown	.25	.05
135,125,000	6¢ Women's Suffrage—Blue	.20	.05
171,850,000	6¢ 150th anniversary of Maine Statehood—Multicolored	.20	.05
135,895,000	6¢ 300th anniversary of English Settlement in South Carolina—Brown, black and red	.20	.05
142,205,000	6¢ Wildlife Conservation, American Buffalo—Brown	.20	.05

Anti-Pollution Issue:

40,400,000	6¢ Save our Soil—Multicolored	$ .85	$ .07
40,400,000	6¢ Save our Cities—Multicolored	.85	.07
40,400,000	6¢ Save our Water—Multicolored	.85	.07
40,400,000	6¢ Save our Air—Multicolored	.85	.07
132,675,000	6¢ Stone Mountain Memorial—Gray	.20	.05
134,795,000	6¢ 150th Anniversary of Fort Snelling—Multicolored	.20	.05
127,610,000	6¢ United Nations—Red, blue and black	.20	.05
129,785,000	6¢ Landing of the Pilgrims—Multicolored	.25	.05

Disabled American Veterans and Servicemen Issue:

72,190,000	6¢ 50 Years of Service—Multicolored ..	$ .35	$ .05
72,190,000	6¢ U.S. Servicemen—Blue, red and black	.35	.05

Christmas Issue:

*390,000,000	6¢ Nativity—Multicolored	$ .25	$ .05
*390,000,000	6¢ Toy Locomotive—Multicolored	1.00	.10
	Same, Precancelled		1.50
*390,000,000	6¢ Toy Horse on Wheels—Multicolored	1.00	.10
	Same, Precancelled		1.50
*390,000,000	6¢ Man on Mechanical Tricycle—Multi-colored	1.00	.10
	Same, Precancelled		1.50
*390,000,000	6¢ Doll Carriage—Multicolored	1.00	.10
	Same, Precancelled		1.50

1970-1974—Regular Issue

6¢ Eisenhower, USA (with dot)—Blue-gray	$ .15	$ .03
7¢ Benjamin Franklin—Blue	.15	.03
8¢ Eisenhower, USA (no dot)—Black, red, blue-gray ..	.18	.04
8¢ Same, with dot after name (issued in booklets only, with panes of 4, 6, or 8)—Deep claret	.18	.04
8¢ United States Postal Service emblem—Multicolored .	.22	.04
14¢ LaGuardia—Brown	.30	.06
16¢ Ernie Pyle, Journalist—Brown....................	.35	.04
18¢ Dr. Elizabeth Blackwell, First Woman Physician—Violet	.35	.06
21¢ Amadeo Giannini, Banker—Green	.40	.06

1971

136,305,000	6¢ America's Wool—Multicolored	$ .20	$ .05
134,840,000	6¢ Douglas MacArthur—Black, red and blue	.20	.05
130,975,000	6¢ Giving Blood Saves Lives—Light and dark blue	.20	.05
161,235,000	8¢ Missouri Sesquicentennial—Multicolored	.25	.05

Wildlife Conservation Issue:

43,919,900	8¢ Trout—Multicolored	$ .30	$ .10
43,919,900	8¢ Alligator—Multicolored	.30	.10
43,919,900	8¢ Polar Bear—Multicolored	.30	.10
43,919,900	8¢ California Condor—Multicolored	.30	.10

138,700,000	8¢ Antarctic Treaty 1961-1971—Red and blue	$ .25	$ .05
138,165,000	8¢ Emblem of American Revolution Bicentennial 1776-1976—Multicolored	.75	.06
152,125,000	8¢ Painting by John Sloan, American Artist—Multicolored	.25	.05

Decade of Space Achievement Issue Twin Stamps:

88,147,500	8¢ Moonscape with Landing Craft—Multicolored	$ .35	$ .10

UNITED STATES IN SPACE··· •A DECADE OF ACHIEVEMENT

| 88,147,500 | 8¢ Moonscape with Astronauts in Lunar Rover—Multicolored | .35 | .10 |
| | Pair | .75 | .35 |

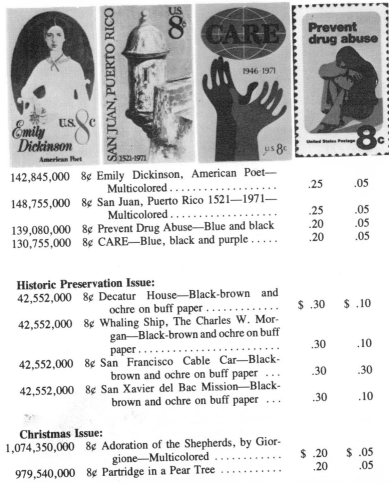

142,845,000	8¢ Emily Dickinson, American Poet—Multicolored	.25	.05
148,755,000	8¢ San Juan, Puerto Rico 1521—1971—Multicolored	.25	.05
139,080,000	8¢ Prevent Drug Abuse—Blue and black	.20	.05
130,755,000	8¢ CARE—Blue, black and purple	.20	.05

Historic Preservation Issue:

42,552,000	8¢ Decatur House—Black-brown and ochre on buff paper	$ .30	$ .10
42,552,000	8¢ Whaling Ship, The Charles W. Morgan—Black-brown and ochre on buff paper	.30	.10
42,552,000	8¢ San Francisco Cable Car—Black-brown and ochre on buff paper	.30	.30
42,552,000	8¢ San Xavier del Bac Mission—Black-brown and ochre on buff paper	.30	.10

Christmas Issue:

| 1,074,350,000 | 8¢ Adoration of the Shepherds, by Giorgione—Multicolored | $ .20 | $ .05 |
| 979,540,000 | 8¢ Partridge in a Pear Tree | .20 | .05 |

1972

137,355,000	8¢ Sidney Lanier, American Poet—Multicolored	$ .20	$ .05
150,400,000	8¢ Peace Corps—Dark and light blue and red	.20	.05
153,025,000	8¢ Family Planning—Multicolored	.20	.05

National Parks Centennial Issue:

43,182,500	2¢ Cape Hatteras, with Seagulls—Multicolored	$ .10	$ .04
43,182,500	2¢ Same, with Lighthouse—Multicolored	.10	.04
43,182,500	2¢ Same, Seashore with Birds—Multicolored	.10	.04
43,182,500	2¢ Same, Seashore with Reeds—Multicolored	.10	.04
104,090,000	6¢ Wolf Trap Farms, Virginia—Multicolored	.20	.04
164,096,000	8¢ Old Faithful, Yellowstone—Multicolored	.20	.05
	11¢ (See airmail stamps)		
53,920,000	15¢ Mount McKinley, Alaska—Multicolored	.40	.15

Colonial American Craftsmen Issue (see Illus. p. 139)

50,472,500	8¢ Glassblower—Brown on buff paper	$ .30	$ .06
50,472,500	8¢ Silversmith—Brown on buff paper	.30	.06
50,472,500	8¢ Wigmaker—Brown on buff paper	.30	.06
50,472,500	8¢ Hatter—Brown on buff paper	.30	.06

Olympic Games Issue: 11¢ (See airmail stamps)

67,335,000	6¢ Summer Games, Bicycling—Multicolored	$ .20	$ .04
179,675,000	8¢ Winter Games, Bobsledding—Multicolored	.22	.05
46,340,000	15¢ Summer Games, Running—Multicolored	.35	.15

180,155,000	8¢ Parent Teacher Association—Black and yellow	.20	.05
185,490,000	8¢ 100th Anniversary of Mail Order—Multicolored	.20	.05
162,235,000	8¢ Osteopathic Medicine—Multicolored	.20	.05
162,789,950	8¢ Tom Sawyer (American Folklore Issue)—Multicolored	.20	.05

Wildlife Conservation Issue:

49,591,200	8¢ Fur Seals—Multicolored	$ .30	$ .05
49,591,200	8¢ Cardinal—Multicolored	.30	.05
49,591,200	8¢ Brown Pelican—Multicolored	.30	.05
49,591,200	8¢ Bighorn Sheep—Multicolored	.30	.05
165,895,000	8¢ Pharmacy—Multicolored	.20	.05
166,508,000	8¢ Stamp Collecting—Multicolored	.20	.05

Christmas Issue:

1,003,475,000	8¢ Angels, Master of St. Lucy Legend—Multicolored...................	$ .20	$ .04
1,017,025,000	8¢ Santa Claus, " 'Twas the Night Before Christmas"—Multicolored ...	.20	.04

1973

328,440,000	8¢ LOVE—Red, green and blue	$ .20	$ .05

Rise of the Spirit of Independence Issue:

166,005,000	8¢ Pamphleteer—Multicolored	$ .25	$ .05
162,800,000	8¢ Posting a Broadside—Multicolored ..	.25	.05
158,880,000	8¢ Post Rider—Multicolored	.25	.05
146,545,000	8¢ Colonial Drummer—Multicolored ...	.25	.05

Boston Tea Party Issue:

48,867,500	8¢ Tea tossed overboard—Multicolored .	$ .25	$ .05
48,867,500	8¢ British Three-master—Multicolored..	.25	.05
48,867,500	8¢ Small boats near ship—Multicolored .	.25	.05
48,867,500	8¢ Small boat approaching dock—Multicolored	.25	.05

American Arts Issue:

132,152,000	8¢ George Gershwin—Multicolored	$ .25	$ .05
128,048,000	8¢ Robinson Jeffers—Multicolored	.25	.05
146,008,000	8¢ Henry O. Tanner—Multicolored	.25	.05
139,608,000	8¢ Willa Cather—Multicolored	.25	.05

157,052,800	8¢ Harry S. Truman—Red, black and blue........................	.20	.05
159,475,000	8¢ Copernicus—Black and orange	.20	.05

U.S. Postal Service Employees Issue:

48,602,000	8¢ Stamp Counter—Multicolored	$ .20	$ .05
48,602,000	8¢ Collecting Mail—Multicolored	.20	.05
48,602,000	8¢ Letters on Conveyor Belt—Multicolored	.20	.05
48,602,000	8¢ Sorting Parcel Post—Multicolored ...	.20	.05
48,602,000	8¢ Canceling Mail—Multicolored	.20	.05
48,602,000	8¢ Manual Letter Routing—Multicolored	.20	.05
48,602,000	8¢ Electronic Letter Routing—Multicolored	.20	.05
48,602,000	8¢ Loading Mail on Truck—Multicolored	.20	.05
48,602,000	8¢ Mailman on Route—Multicolored ...	.20	.05
48,602,000	8¢ Rural Mail Delivery—Multicolored ..	.20	.05

Progress in Electronics Issue:

53,005,000	6¢ Marconi Spark Coil and Spark Gap—Multicolored		$ .15	$ .04
159,775,000	8¢ Transistors—Multicolored		.20	.05
	11¢ (See airmail stamps)			
39,005,000	15¢ Microphone, Radio Tube, TV Camera Tube, Radio Speaker—Multicolored		.35	.15

Rural America Issue:

145,840,000	8¢ Angus Cattle—Multicolored		$ .20	$ .05
	10¢ Chautauqua 1874-1974, Tent—Multicolored		.25	.05
	10¢ Kansas Hard Winter Wheat—Multicolored		.25	.05

152,624,000	8¢ Lyndon B. Johnson—Multicolored ..	.20	.05

Christmas Issue:

885,160,000 8¢ Raphael Madonna—Multicolored . . . . $ .20 $ .04
939,835,000 8¢ Christmas Tree—Multicolored . . . . . . .20 .04

1973-74—Regular Issue:

10¢ 50-Star and 13-Star Crossed Flags—Red, white and
blue . . . . $ .20 $ .03
10¢ Jefferson Memorial Monument—Blue . . . . .20 .03
10¢ It All Depends on Zip Code—Multicolored . . . . .20 .03
6.3¢ Liberty Bell—Red and white (coil stamp for bulk
mail) . . . . .15 .07

1974

143,930,000 10¢ V.F.W.—Red and blue . . . . $ .25 $ .05
140,150,000 10¢ Robert Frost, American Poet—Black
and white . . . . .25 .05
127,116,000 10¢ Expo '74, Preserve the Environment—
Multicolored . . . . .25 .05

141,740,000 10¢ Horse Racing—Multicolored . . . . .25 .05
160,280,000 10¢ Skylab IV—Multicolored . . . . .25 .05
136,575,000 10¢ First Kentucky Settlement, Fort Har-
rod—Multicolored . . . . .25 .05

Universal Postal Union Issue:

19,614,800	10¢	Michelangelo—Multicolored	$ .25	$ .05
19,614,800	10¢	Hokusai painting—Multicolored	.25	.05
19,614,800	10¢	"Old Scraps"—Multicolored	.25	.05
19,614,800	10¢	"The Lovely Reader"—Multicolored	.25	.05
19,614,800	10¢	Lady Writing Letter—Multicolored ..	.25	.05
19,614,800	10¢	Inkwell and Quill—Multicolored	.25	.05
19,614,800	10¢	Gainsborough Painting—Multicolored	.25	.05
19,614,800	10¢	Goya Painting—Multicolored	.25	.05

Mineral Heritage Issue:

37,016,250	10¢ Petrified Wood—Multicolored		$ .25	$ .05
37,016,250	10¢ Tourmaline—Multicolored		.25	.05
37,016,250	10¢ Amethyst—Multicolored		.25	.05
37,016,250	10¢ Rhodochrosite—Multicolored		.25	.05

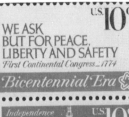

First Continental Congress Issue:

34,903,750	10¢ Carpenter's Hall—Red, blue and gray	$ .25	$ .05
34,903,750	10¢ "We Ask but for Peace, Liberty and Safety"—Red, blue and gray	.25	.05
34,903,750	10¢ "Deriving Their Just Powers From the Consent of the Governed"—Red, blue and gray	.25	.05
34,903,750	10¢ Independence Hall—Red, blue and gray	.25	.05
148,850,000	10¢ Energy Conservation—Multicolored	.25	.05

157,270,000	10¢ The Legend of Sleepy Hollow (American Folklore Issue)—Multicolored	.25	.05

150,245,000	10¢	Retarded Children Can Be Helped—Brown	.25	.05

Christmas Issue (see Illus. p. 145)

835,180,000	10¢	Angel, Altarpiece—Multicolored	$ .25	$ .05
882,520,000	10¢	"The Road—Winter," by Currier and Ives—Multicolored	.25	.05
*230,000,000	10¢	Dove of Peace Weathervane at Mount Vernon (no perforations, self-adhesive, precancelled)—Multicolored .		.20

1975

153,355,000	10¢	Collective Bargaining—Multicolored	$ .25	$ .04

Unmanned Space Probe Issue:

173,685,000	10¢	Mariner 10, Venus/Mercury—Multicolored	$ .25	$ .04
158,600,000	10¢	Pioneer, Jupiter—Multicolored	.25	.04

American Arts Issue:

156,995,000	10¢	Benjamin West, American Artist—Multicolored...................	$ .25	$ .04
146,365,000	10¢	Paul Laurence Dunbar, American Poet—Multicolored	.25	.04
148,805,000	10¢	D. W. Griffith, Moviemaker—Multicolored	.25	.04

Revolutionary Battles:

144,028,000	10¢	Lexington and Concord 1775	$ .25	$ .04
139,928,000	10¢	Bunker Hill 1775	.25	.04

146

Sybil Ludington 🏵 *Youthful Heroine*

Haym Salomon 🏵 *Financial Hero*

Salem Poor 🏵 *Gallant Soldier*

Peter Francisco 🏵 *Fighter Extraordinary*

Contributors to the Cause Issue:

63,205,000	8¢ Sybil Ludington, Youthful Heroine— Multicolored	$ .20	$ .04
157,865,000	10¢ Haym Salomon, Financial Hero— Multicolored	.25	.04
166,810,000	10¢ Salem Poor, Gallant Soldier	.25	.04
44,825,000	18¢ Peter Francisco, Fighter Extraordinary	.50	.05

Continental Military Uniforms Issue:

179,855,000	10¢ Continental Army Uniform—Multi- colored	$ .20	$ .05
179,855,000	10¢ Continental Navy Uniform—Multico- lored	.20	.05
179,855,000	10¢ Continental Marine Uniform—Multi- colored	.20	.05
179,855,000	10¢ American Militia Uniform—Multicol- ored	.20	.05

Apollo-Soyuz Space Issue:

161,863,200	10¢ Apollo and Soyuz After Docking, Earth in Background—Multicolored	$ .25	$ .10
161,863,200	10¢ Spacecrafts Prior To Docking, Earth and Project Insignia—Multicolored	.25	.10
	Pair..........................	.50	.20
145,640,000	10¢ International Women's Year—Blue, orange and dark blue	.20	.04

U.S. Postal Service Bicentennial Issue:

168,655,000 10¢ Stagecoach and Trailer Truck—Multicolored	$ .20	$ .05
168,655,000 10¢ Old and New Locomotives—Multicolored	.20	.05
168,655,000 10¢ Vintage Mail Plane and Jet—Multicolored	.20	.05
168,655,000 10¢ Satellite for Transmitting Mailgrams—Multicolored	.20	.05
146,615,000 10¢ World Peace Through Law—Multicolored	.20	.04

Banking and Commerce Issue:

146,196,000 10¢ Engine Turning, Indian Head Cent and Morgan Dollar—Multicolored	$ .25	$ .08
146,196,000 10¢ Liberty Quarter, $20 Gold Piece and Engine Turning—Multicolored	.25	.08
Pair	.50	.20

Christmas Issue

739,430,000 10¢ Madonna, by Domenico Ghirlandaio—Multicolored	$ .20	$ .04
878,690,000 10¢ Early Christmas Card, by Louis Prang—Multicolored	.20	.04

1975-79—Americana Issue:

1¢ Inkwell and Quill Pen—Blue on greenish	$ .03	$ .03
1¢ Same, Precancelled		.04
2¢ Speaker's Stand—Red brown on greenish	.04	.03
2¢ Same, Precancelled		.04
3¢ Vintage Ballot Box—Olive on greenish	.05	.03
3¢ Same, Precancelled		.04
4¢ Books, Bookmark, Spectacles—Rose magenta on cream	.07	.03
4¢ Same, Precancelled		.03
9¢ Dome of U.S. Capitol—Slate green. Size, 17½ × 20½mm. (Issued in booklets only. All stamps have one or two straight edges.)	.18	.03
9¢ Same—Slate green on gray. Size 18½ × 22½mm ..	.18	.03
9¢ Same, Precancelled		.06
10¢ Contemplation of Justice—Violet on gray	.20	.03
11¢ Early American Printing Press—Orange on gray	.22	.03
13¢ Liberty Bell—Brown (Issued in booklets only, with panes of 5, 6, 7, or 8.)	.26	.03
13¢ U.S. Eagle and Shield—Multicolored	.26	.03

15¢ Fort McHenry Flag—Gray, dark blue and red	.30	.03
15¢ Same (Issued in booklets only, pane of 8.)	.30	.03
16¢ Head, Statue of Liberty—Blue	.32	.03
24¢ Old North Church, Boston—Red on blue	.48	.04
28¢ Fort Nisqually—Brown on blue	.56	.04
29¢ Sandy Hook Lighthouse, N.J.—Blue on blue	.58	.04
30¢ American Schools—Green on green	.60	.04
50¢ Iron "Betty" Lamp—Black and orange on buff	1.00	.10
$1 Rush Lamp and Candleholder—Black, yellow and orange on buff	2.00	.15
$2 Kerosene Table Lamp—Dark green and orange on buff	4.00	.75
$5 Railroad Conductor's Lantern—Red brown, yellow and orange on buff.........................	7.50	1.25

Coil Stamps:
Perforated 10 Vertically
(Bulk Rate Postage)

3.1¢	Six-string guitar—brown on canary	$ .07	$ .03
3.1¢	Same, Precancelled		.03
7.7¢	Saxhorns—Gold on yellow	.16	.03
7.7¢	Same, Precancelled		.04
7.9¢	Drum—Red on yellow	.16	.03
7.9¢	Same, Precancelled		.04
8.4¢	Piano—Dark blue on yellow....................	.17	.03
8.4¢	Same, Precancelled		.04
9¢	Dome of U.S. Capitol—Slate green on gray	.18	.03
9¢	Same, Precancelled...........................		.06
10¢	Contemplation of Justice—Violet on gray	.20	.03
10¢	Same, Precancelled...........................		.07
13¢	Liberty Bell—Brown	.26	.03
13¢	Same, Precancelled...........................		.08
15¢	Fort McHenry Flag—Gray, dark blue and red	.30	.04
16¢	Head, Statue of Liberty—Blue	.32	.04

Multicolor Huck Press:
Perforated 11 × 10½

13¢	13-Star Flag, Independence Hall—Dark blue and red	$ .26	$ .03
13¢	Flag over U.S. Capitol—Blue and red (Issued in Booklets only.)	.26	.03
13¢	13-Star Flag, Independence Hall—Dark blue and red (Same as above; issued as a coil stamp.)	.26	.03

1976
U.S. Bicentennial—"Spirit of '76" Issue

219,455,000	13¢	Drummer Boy—Multicolored	$ .30	$ .08
219,455,000	13¢	Older Drummer—Multicolored	.30	.08
219,455,000	13¢	Fifer—Multicolored	.30	.08
		Strip of three	1.00	.40
157,825,000	13¢	"Interphil '76"—Dark blue, red and ultramarine	.30	.06

State Flags Issue

436,005,000	Sheet of fifty 13¢ values portraying all the state flags, arranged according to the date of the state's admission to the Union: from Delaware to Hawaii. ....

$.50 (mint singles)
.35 (used singles)
25.00 (mint sheet of 50)

159,915,000	13¢ Telephone Centennial, Bell—Black, purple and red on tan	$ .30	$ .04
156,960,000	13¢ Commercial Aviation 1926-1976— Blue and multicolored	.30	.04
158,470,000	13¢ American Chemistry Society Centennial—Multicolored	.30	.04

Washington Crossing the Delaware
From a Painting by Emanuel Leutze / Eastman Johnson

U.S. Bicentennial Issue
Souvenir Sheets

At Philadelphia's "Interphil '76," the United States, on May 29, 1976, issued four large souvenir sheets with Bicentennial themes. Reproduced on the sheets are details from famous paintings depicting events of the Revolutionary period. Overprinting and perforations permit five portions of each sheet to be removed and used as postage stamps. However, very few of these stamps were actually used in the mails.

1,990,000	65¢ (Sheet of five 13¢ values) "Surrender of Cornwallis at Yorktown," by John Trumbull—multicolored	$5.00

1,983,000	90¢ (Sheet of five 18¢ values) "Declaration of Independence," by John Trumbull—multicolored	7.50	
1,953,000	$1.20 (Sheet of five 24¢ values) "Washington Crossing the Delaware," by Emmanuel Leutze/Eastman Johnson—multicolored .	10.00	
1,903,000	$1.55 (Sheet of five 31¢ values) "Washington Reviewing His Ragged Army at Valley Forge," by William T. Trego—multicolored	15.00	
164,890,000	13¢ Benjamin Franklin, Map of North America in 1776 (U.S. Bicentennial Issue)—Ultramarine and multicolored	.30	.04

JULY 4, 1776 ⸱ JULY 4, 1776 ⸱ JULY 4, 1776 ⸱ JULY 4, 1776

U.S. Bicentennial Issue
Strip of Four 13¢ Values Depicting Artist John Trumbull's "Declaration of Independence"

204,035,000	13¢ Multicolored	$ .30	$ .06
204,035,000	13¢ Multicolored	.30	.06
204,035,000	13¢ Multicolored	.30	.06
204,035,000	13¢ Multicolored	.30	.06
	Strip of four....................	1.50	.30

Olympic Games Issue:

185,715,000	13¢ Diving—Multicolored	$ .30	$ .06
185,715,000	13¢ Cross-Country Skiing—Multicolored .	.30	.06
185,715,000	13¢ Running—Multicolored	.30	.06
185,715,000	13¢ Ice Skating—Multicolored	.30	.06
130,592,000	13¢ Clara Maass, Nurse—Multicolored ..	.30	.04
158,332,800	13¢ Adolph S. Ochs, Publisher—Black and gray	.30	.04

Christmas Issue:

809,955,000	13¢ "Nativity," by John Singleton Copley—Multicolored	$ .30	$ .04
963,370,000	13¢ "Winter Pastime," by Nathaniel Currier—Multicolored	.30	.04
	13¢ Same, Photogravure	.30	.04

1977

153,028,000	13¢ "Washington at Princeton," by Charles Willson Peale (U.S. Bicentennial Issue)—Multicolored	$ .30	$ .05
176,805,000	13¢ Sound Recording Centennial, Edison—Black and Multicolored	.30	.04

American Folk Art Issue
Pueblo Indian Pottery:

195,848,000	13¢ Zia Pot—Multicolored	$ .30	$ .05
195,848,000	13¢ San Ildefonso Pot—Multicolored	.30	.05
195,848,000	13¢ Hopi Pot—Multicolored	.30	.05
195,848,000	13¢ Acoma Pot—Multicolored	.30	.05
208,820,000	13¢ Lindbergh Transatlantic Flight 1927-1977—Multicolored	.30	.05
190,005,000	13¢ Colorado Statehood Centennial—Multicolored	.30	.04

Butterfly Issue:

218,885,000	13¢ Swallowtail—Tan and multicolored	$ .30	$ .05
218,885,000	13¢ Checkerspot—Tan and multicolored	.30	.05
218,885,000	13¢ Dogface—Tan and multicolored	.30	.05
218,885,000	13¢ Orange Tip—Tan and multicolored	.30	.05

159,772,000 13¢ Lafayette (U.S. Bicentennial Issue)—
Blue, black and red 30   .05

U.S. Bicentennial Issue
Skilled Hands for Independence
184,780,000 13¢ Seamstress—Multicolored	$ .30	$ .06
184,780,000 13¢ Blacksmith—Multicolored	.30	.06
184,780,000 13¢ Wheelright—Multicolored	.30	.06
184,780,000 13¢ Leatherworker—Multicolored	.30	.06

163,230,000 13¢ Peace Bridge, U.S.-Canada—Blue ..   .30   .05
155,828,000 13¢ Battle of Oriskany (U.S. Bicentennial
Issue)—Multicolored 30   .05

Energy Issue:
158,008,000 13¢ "Energy Conservation"—Multicol-
ored . . . . $ .30 $ .05
158,008,000 13¢ "Energy Development"—Multicol-
ored 30   .05
Pair. 60   .10

154,495,000 13¢ Alta, California—Black and multicolored 30   .05
160,590,000 13¢ Articles of Confederation (U.S. Bicentennial Issue)—Red and brown
on cream 30   .05
155,225,000 13¢ Talking Pictures 1927-1977—Multicolored 30   .05
153,672,000 13¢ "Surrender of Burgoyne," by John
Trumbull (U.S. Bicentennial
Issue)—Multicolored 30   .05

Christmas Issue:
882,260,000 13¢ Washington at Valley Forge—Multicolored . . . . $ .30 $ .04
921,530,000 13¢ Rural Mailbox—Multicolored 30   .04

1978
13¢ Carl Sandburg—Black and brown . . . . $ .30 $ .05

Captain Cook Issue:
13¢ Cook Portrait, by Nathaniel Dance—Dark blue . . . . . $ .30 $ .06
13¢ "Resolution" and "Discovery," by John Webber—
Green 30   .06
Pair 60   .12

13¢ Indian Head Cent, 1877—Brown and blue green on bistre ..... :	.30	.03
(15¢) Eagle (no value indicated)—Orange	.30	.03
15¢ Roses—Multicolored	.30	.03
15¢ Harriet Tubman (Black Heritage Issue)—Multicolored	.30	.05

American Folk Art Issue
American Quilts, Basket Design

13¢ Multicolored	$ .30	$ .06
13¢ Multicolored	.30	.06
13¢ Multicolored	.30	.06
13¢ Multicolored	.30	.06

American Dance Issue:

13¢ Ballet—Multicolored	$ .30	$ .06
13¢ Theatrical Dance—Multicolored	.30	.06
13¢ Folk Dance—Multicolored	.30	.06
13¢ Modern Dance—Multicolored	.30	.06

13¢ Franco-American Alliance (U.S. Bicentennial Issue)—Multicolored	.30	.05
13¢ Early Cancer Detection, Pap Test—Brown	.30	.05

Performing Arts Issue:

13¢ Jimmie Rodgers, the "Singing Brakesman"—Multicolored	$ .30	$ .05
15¢ George M. Cohan, "Yankee Doodle Dandy"—Multicolored	.30	.05

Canadian International Philatelic Exhibition
Toronto

This tribute features wildlife that share the Canadian-United States border.

*Cette émission souvenir est consacrée à la faune vivant près
de la frontière entre les Etats-Unis et le Canada.*

Postmaster General of the United States

CAPEX (Canadian International Philatelic Exhibition, Toronto) Issue:

13¢ Cardinal	$ .30	$ .08
13¢ Mallard	.30	.08
13¢ Canada Goose	.30	.08
13¢ Blue Jay	.30	.08
13¢ Moose	.30	.08
13¢ Chipmunk	.30	.08
13¢ Red Fox	.30	.08
13¢ Raccoon	.30	.08
15¢ Photography—Multicolored	.30	.05
15¢ Viking Missions to Mars—Multicolored	.30	.05

American Owls Issue:

15¢ Great Gray Owl—Multicolored	$ .30	$ .06
15¢ Saw-whet Owl—Multicolored	.30	.06
15¢ Barred Owl—Multicolored	.30	.06
15¢ Great Horned Owl—Multicolored	.30	.06

American Trees Issue:

15¢ Giant Sequoia—Multicolored	$ .30	$ .06
15¢ White Pine—Multicolored	.30	.06
15¢ White Oak—Multicolored	.30	.06
15¢ Gray Birch—Multicolored	.30	.06

Christmas Issue:

15¢ Madonna and Child with Cherubs, by Andrea della Robbia—Blue and multicolored .... $ .30 $ .04
15¢ Little Boy on Hobby Horse and Christmas Trees—Red and multicolored 30   .04

1979

15¢ Robert F. Kennedy—Blue .... $ .30 $ .04
15¢ Martin Luther King, Jr. (Black Heritage Issue)—Multicolored 30   .04
15¢ International Year of the Child—Orange-red 30   .04
15¢ John Steinbeck—Dark blue 30   .04
15¢ Albert Einstein—Chocolate 30   .04

American Folk Art Issue
Pennsylvania Toleware

15¢ Coffeepot:—Multicolored .... $ .30 $ .06
15¢ Tea Caddy—Multicolored 30   .06
15¢ Sugar Bowl—Multicolored 30   .06
15¢ Coffeepot—Multicolored 30   .06

American Architecture Issue:

15¢ Virginia Rotunda, by Thomas Jefferson—Black and brick red .... $ .30 $ .06
15¢ Baltimore Cathedral, by Benjamin Latrobe—Black and brick red 30   .06
15¢ Boston State House, by Charles Bulfinch—Black and brick red 30   .06
15¢ Philadelphia Exchange by William Strickland—Black and brick red 30   .06

Endangered Flora Issue:

15¢ Persistent Trillium—Multicolored .... $ .30 $ .06
15¢ Hawaiian Wild Broadbeam—Multicolored 30   .06
15¢ Contra Costa Wallflower—Multicolored 30   .06
15¢ Antioch Dunes Evening Primrose—Multicolored 30   .06

15¢ Seeing Eye Dog, "Seeing For Me"—Multicolored ..	.30	.04
15¢ Special Olympics, "Skill-Sharing-Joy"—Multicolored	.30	.04
10¢ Olympics Decathlon—Multicolored	.20	.04
15¢ John Paul Jones (U.S. Bicentennial Issue)—Multicolored	.30	.05

1980 Olympics Summer Events Series:

15¢ Running—Multicolored	$ .30	$ .05
15¢ Swimming—Multicolored	.30	.05
15¢ Rowing—Multicolored	.30	.05
15¢ Horsemanship—Multicolored	.30	.05

Christmas Issue:

15¢ Madonna and Child, by Gerard David	$ .30	$ .04
15¢ Santa Claus—Multicolored	.30	.04
15¢ Will Rogers (Performing Arts Issue)—Multicolored .	.30	.04
15¢ Honoring Vietnam Veterans—Multicolored	.30	.04

UNITED STATES AIR MAIL STAMPS

1918

3,395,854	6¢ Curtis Biplane—Orange	$125.00	$27.50
3,793,887	16¢ Same—Green	185.00	37.50
2,134,888	24¢ Same—Red, blue	175.00	37.50
	24¢ Same, inverted center (airplane upside down!) (see Illus. p. 54)	130,000.00	

1923

6,414,576	8¢ Propeller and airplane nose—Green..	$50.00	$17.50
5,309,275	16¢ Air Service emblem—Blue.........	150.00	35.00
5,285,775	24¢ Biplane—Red	175.00	25.00

1926-27

42,092,800	10¢ Map of U.S. and Mail Planes—Blue	$6.50	$ .50
15,597,307	15¢ Same—Brown	7.50	2.75
17,616,350	20¢ Same—Green	20.00	2.50

1927

20,379,179	10¢ "Spirit of St. Louis" and Route of Lindbergh's Flight—Blue	$15.00	$3.50

1928

106,887,675	5¢ Beacon on Rocky Mountains—Blue and red	$7.50	$ .65

1930-39

154,981,250	5¢ Winged Globe—Violet	$17.50	$ .50
302,205,000	6¢ Same—Orange	1.75	.10
76,648,803	8¢ Same—Olive green	2.00	.25
19,768,150	30¢ Same, Trans-Atlantic—Blue	17.50	1.20

1930

Graf Zeppelin Issue (see Illus. p. 50):

93,536	65¢ Zeppelin over the Atlantic—Green	$750.00	$275.00
72,428	$1.30 Zeppelin between Continents—Brown	1,500.00	500.00
61,296	$2.60 Zeppelin passing Globe—Blue	2,000.00	750.00

1933

324,070 50¢ Zeppelin, Century of Progress Flight—
Green (See Illus. p. 51) $175.00 $75.00

1935-37

Trans-Pacific Clipper Issue:

12,794,600	20¢ Clipper over the Pacific—Green	$22.50	$2.50
10,205,400	25¢ Same—Blue	2.75	1.75
9,285,300	50¢ Same—Red	20.00	5.50

1938

349,946,500 6¢ Eagle and Shield—Red, blue .... $ .65 $ .10

1941-46

4,746,527,700	5¢ Twin-Motored Transport—Red	$ .20	$ .05
1,744,878,650	8¢ Same—Olive green	.30	.05
67,117,400	10¢ Same—Violet	1.35	.15
78,434,800	15¢ Same—Brown	2.50	.30
42,359,850	20¢ Same—Green	2.25	.25
59,880,850	30¢ Same—Blue..................	3.00	.30
11,160,600	50¢ Same—Orange	20.00	3.50
864,753,100	5¢ Four-Motored Transport—Red	.15	.04

1947-49

971,903,700	5¢ Four-Motored Transport, small size—Red	$ .18	$ .04
5,070,095,200	6¢ Same—Red	.20	.03

207,976,550	10¢ Pan-American Building—Black	.40	.06
756,186,350	15¢ New York Skyline—Green.........	.50	.06
132,956,100	25¢ Oakland Bay Bridge—Blue	1.35	.12

1948

38,449,100	5¢ New York City Jubilee Issue—Red ..	$ .25	$ .15

1949

75,085,000	6¢ Alexandria, Virginia Bicentennial—Red......................	$ .20	$ .10
80,405,000	6¢ Wright Brothers and their plane—Magenta.......................	.25	.10

Universal Postal Union Anniversary Issue (see Illus. p. 17):

21,061,300	10¢ Post Office Building in Washington—Violet	$ .50	$ .30
36,613,100	15¢ Globe and Doves—Blue	.65	.50
16,217,100	25¢ Plane and Globe—Red	1.10	.60

1952
18,876,800   80¢ Diamond Head, Hawaii—Red violet . $8.75 $1.25
1953
78,415,000   6¢ 50th Anniversary of Flight—Red .... $ .20 $ .10
1954
50,483,600   4¢ Eagle in Flight—Blue . . . . $ .15 $ .08

1957
63,185,000   6¢ U.S.A.F., 50th Anniversary—Blue .. $ .20 $ .09
1958
72,480,000   5¢ Eagle in Flight—Red . . . . $ .22 $ .10
1,326,960,000   7¢ Jet—Blue 25   .04

1959
90,055,200   7¢ Alaska Statehood—Blue . . . . $ .25 $ .10
79,290,000   7¢ Balloon Jupiter—Blue and red 25   .10
            (see Illus. p. 49) . . . .
84,815,000   7¢ Hawaii Statehood—Red 25   .10
38,770,000   10¢ Pan-American Games—Blue and red   .65   .40

98,160,000	15¢ Statue of Liberty—Black and orange	.85	.10

1960

39,960,000	10¢ Liberty Bell—Black and green......	$2.75	$ .50
	25¢ Lincoln—Black and maroon........	.65	.10

1,289,460,000	7¢ Jet—Red	.30	.05

1961

13¢ Liberty Bell—Black and red	$ .50	$ .10
15¢ Statue of Liberty (Revised, no frame line)—Black and orange	.50	.10

1962

8¢ Plane and Capitol Dome—Carmine	$ .22	$ .04

1963

42,245,000 (see Illus. p. 17)	15¢ Montgomery Blair, Chain of Letters and Globe, First International Postal Conference Centenary—Dull red, dark brown and blue	$1.65	$ .45
	6¢ Bald Eagle (Postal card rate)—Red ..	.20	.08
63,890,000	8¢ Amelia Earhart and Plane—Carmine and maroon	.35	.10

1964

62,255,000	8¢ Dr. Goddard, Rocket and Tower—Blue, red and bistre	$1.10	$ .15

1967

55,710,000	8¢ Totem Pole, Alaska Purchase Centenary—Dark brown	$ .75	$ .12
*50,000,000	20¢ "Columbia" Jays—Blue, brown and bistre	1.20	.20

1968

	10¢ 50 stars—Carmine	$ .25	$ .04
	$1 Eagle with Pennant (Issued primarily for reduced-rate airmail parcels to armed forces overseas)—Lake-brown, deep blue and yellow buff	3.50	2.00
*60,000,000	10¢ Curtis Jenny Biplane, 50th Anniversary of Airmail Service—Black, blue and red	.65	.10
	20¢ Letters "U.S.A." and Plane—Red, blue and black . .	.85	.07

1969

152,364,000	10¢ Astronaut stepping onto Moon's Surface—Red, blue and brown (see Illus. p. 58)	$ .40	$ .10

1971-73

9¢	Delta Wing Plane—Red	$ .20	$ .09
11¢	Jet Airliner—Carmine.........................	.25	.04
13¢	Winged Airmail Envelope—Carmine	.30	.04

17¢	Head of Statue of Liberty—Multicolored	.45	.15
21¢	Letters "U.S.A." and Plane—Red, blue and black (see Illus. p. 153)...........................	.45	.15

1972

78,210,000 11¢	City of Refuge, Hawaii (National Parks Centennial Issue)—Multicolored ..	$ .30	$ .08
96,240,000 11¢	Olympic Winter Games, Sapporo 1972, Skiing—Multicolored	.25	.08

1973

58,705,000 11¢	DeForest Audions (Progress in Electronics Issue)—Multicolored	$ .30	$ .08

1974

18¢ Statue of Liberty—Red, black and blue .... $ .45 $ .15
26¢ Shrine of Democracy, Mt. Rushmore—Blue, black
and red .... .60 .15

1976

25¢ Airplane and Globes—Ultramarine, red and black ... $ .50 $ .10
31¢ Airplane, Globes and Flag—Ultramarine, red and
black .... .60 .10

1978

Aviation Pioneers Issue
Wright Brothers Issue
31¢ Orville and Wilbur Wright and "Flyer A"—Ultramarine and multicolored .... $ .60 $ .10
31¢ Wright Brothers, "Flyer A" and Shed—Ultramarine
and multicolored .... .60 .10

166

1979

Aviation Pioneers Issue
Octave Chanute Issue

21¢ Chanute and Biplane Hang-glider—Multicolored	$ .40	$ .10
21¢ Biplane Hang-gliders and Chanute—Multicolored ...	.40	.10
Aviation Pioneers Issue		
25¢ Wiley Post and the "Winnie Mae"—Multicolored ..	$ .50	$ .10
25¢ Wiley Post in "Altitude Suit," and the "Winnie Mae"—Multicolored	.50	.10
31¢ Olympics Highjumper—Multicolored	.60	.10
25¢ Wiley Post Issue	.50	.08

UNITED STATES AIR MAIL
SPECIAL DELIVERY ISSUES

1934-36

9,215,750 16¢ Seal of the U.S.—Blue..............	$ .75	$ .65
72,517,850 16¢ Same—Red and blue	.55	.20

UNITED STATES SPECIAL DELIVERY ISSUES

1885-88

10¢ Man running (Inscribed "Immediate delivery at a special delivery office")—Blue $150.00 $22.50

1888

10¢ Man running (Inscribed "Immediate delivery at any post office")—Blue $150.00 $6.25

1893

10¢ Same—Orange $75.00 $8.75

1894-1895

10¢ Man Running (Line under "TEN CENTS") $350.00 $12.50

1902-17

10¢ Man on Bicycle—Blue $37.50 $2.25

1908

10¢ Olive Branch and Helmet—Green $40.00 $17.50

1922-51

10¢	Man and Motorcycle—Blue	$20.00	$ .15
10¢	Same—Violet or violet blue....................	.55	.05
13¢	Same—Blue	.50	.05
15¢	Same—Orange	.60	.08
17¢	Same—Yellow	4.50	1.25

1925

20¢	Post Office Truck—Black	$2.25	$ .85

1954-57

20¢	Letter and Hands—Blue	$ .70	$ .10
30¢	Same—Maroon	.90	.10

1969-71

45¢	Arrows—Red, white and blue	$1.75	$ .12
60¢	Same, blue, white and red	1.15	.12

REGISTRATION STAMP

1911

10¢ Eagle—Blue $80.00 $3.50

CERTIFIED MAIL

1955

15¢ Mailman—Red .... $ .55 $ .30

SPECIAL HANDLING STAMPS

1925-29

10¢ Numeral—Green	$ .75	$ .75
15¢ Same—Green	1.50	.75
20¢ Same—Green	1.85	1.25
25¢ Same—Green	22.50	6.00

PARCEL POST SERIES

1912-13

1¢	Post Office Clerk—Red	$2.50	$ .60
2¢	City Carrier—Red	2.75	.50
3¢	Railway Mail Clerk—Red	6.25	3.00
4¢	Rural Carrier—Red	16.00	1.25
5¢	Mail Train—Red	12.75	.65
10¢	Steamship and Mail Tender—Red	25.00	1.50
15¢	Old time auto—Red	37.50	6.25
20¢	Old time plane—Red	67.50	9.75
25¢	Factory—Red	27.50	3.25
50¢	Dairy Herd—Red	115.00	22.50
75¢	Harvesting—Red	32.50	17.50
$1	Fruit Growing—Red	200.00	15.00

INDEX